STRAIGHT

PUBL

ROBERT FRANKS

Straightforward Guides

© Straightforward Publishing 2017

British Cataloguing in Publication data. A catalogue record is available for this book from the British Library.

ISBN
978-1-84716-705-7

Printed in the United Kingdom by 4Edge www.4edge.co.uk

Cover Design by Bookworks Islington

Whilst every effort has been made to ensure that the information in this book is accurate at the time of going to print, the author and publisher recognise that the information can become out of date. The book is therefore sold on the understanding that no responsibility for errors and omissions is assumed and no responsibility is held for the information held within.

CONTENTS

Table of Cases

Introduction

A Straightforward Guide to Public Law is a wide ranging book covering all the relevant law and practice that constitutes the operation of constitutional and administrative law in the United Kingdom.

The book starts by placing the history of the growth of the constitution in the UK, from the Magna Carta onwards. Within this context, we then examine the actual nature of the British constitution, and its unwritten nature and how it has formed relative to those countries with a written constitution. We look at sources of constitutional law, and the rule of law, examining Dicey's famous exposition.

From this point we look at the administration of government, how it functions, examining the role of Parliament, and the role of the players on a day to day basis plus the formulation and passage of legislation. We also look at Electoral law and how the process of voting works in the UK, which serves to elect those politicians who form the government. The civil service is examined, which is non-elected, along with its functions.

The European Community, its development and impact on public law is outlined and also Human Rights law. Within this context we look at the Referendum to exit the EU BREXIT and its future impact on public law.

The final chapters deal with police organisation and public order, plus the process of judicial review, which gives the right to challenge decisions of public bodies. This brief but comprehensive book should prove invaluable to both students and layperson in understanding the meaning and operations of public law in the United Kingdom.

Ch.1

Public law-The History of the British Constitution

The below represents, not a complete history of The British Constitution, but an overview of key events in history which serve to give a background to the development, meaning and existence of the Constitution and the role it plays in current political life.

To gain an understanding of the development of the British constitution it is necessary to go back more than a thousand years.

Before the Norman conquest of England, what is now recognised as England came about in 927 AD when the last of the Heptarch kingdoms fell under the rule of the English King. Until 1066, and the Battle of Hastings, England was ruled by monarchs who were elected by the *witan* (wise).

Following the Battle of Hastings in 1066, and the Norman invasion, Henry 1ˢᵗ of England came to the throne (1068) When he ascended to the throne he granted the Charter of Liberties. Although this document was not a bill of rights as such it did grant a series of decrees and assurances. The charter, at the outset, states *'that by the mercy of god and the common counsel of the barons of the whole kingdom of England I have been crowned king of the whole kingdom'*

This statement, and its intent, represents a move away from absolute monarchy and a step towards constitutionalism. Essentially, within this statement the king had recognised that the right to rule came not only from god but also from the common counsel of the barons.

The importance of this charter, and this particular point in time, is that the power structure in England evolved from an essentially absolutist model to a constitutional model.

The Plantagenets

The ascension of King John (1167-1216) was another very important milestone in constitutional history. The period of his rule was marked by conflict resulting in the signing of the Magna Carta (Great Charter), which was issued in 1215.

The Magna Carta is of massive importance in that it influenced the development of common law and many other constitutional documents, such as the American Bill of Rights. It was originally written because of disagreements between Pope Innocent 111, King John and the English barons about the rights of the King. Magna Carta required the King to renounce certain specific rights, respect certain legal procedures and accept that his will could be bound by law. It protected certain rights of the King's subjects, most notably the writ of Habeas Corpus, which allowed appeal against unlawful imprisonment. By the late 19th century most of the original clauses had been repealed from English law.

The Magna Carta was the first document forced on an English King, limiting his powers by law. By the time of the Civil war it had become an important symbol for those who wished to show that the King was bound by the law. The actual Magna Carta which remains on the statute books of England and Wales is an amended 1297 version.

Henry the Third succeeded his father and was forced to accept the existence of the first English Parliament.

The Tudors

The first Act of Supremacy (1534) made King Henry V111 the 'supreme head' of the Church of England. The second Act of Supremacy (1559) restored these powers to Elizabeth the 1st, reversing Catholic legislation passed during the reign of Mary, who had sought to overturn it.

The monarchy had to get the consent of Parliament in all issues. In turn, Parliament showed loyalty to the monarch which, however, decreased when the Spanish Armada was defeated (1588) and Parliament felt safe once more. The House of Commons had grown sharply, doubling in size, mainly due to the prosperity of the middle-class during that time.

James V1

When Queen Elizabeth 1st died in 1603 she was succeeded by her cousin James V1 of Scotland, the son of Mary, Queen of Scots, and he became James 1st of England This was a major step in the creation of a United Kingdom. James V1 faced a fractious religious England containing Anglicans, Puritans, Separatists (who wanted to break from the Anglican Church) and Catholics. James V1 was a believer in the Divine Right of Kings Theory which stated that Kings were chosen by God. Though he was a Presbyterian he was against the Presbyterian idea of allowing the congregation (people) to elect their Presbyters (church officials) since it undermined his absolutism.

The Civil War

James was succeeded by his son who became Charles 1st in 1625. He also believed in Divine Right Theory and continued to fight with

Parliament. The Parliaments main power at this time was its control of taxes. Traditionally, Parliament had voted at the start of a Kings reign on the amount allowed for the King's Tonnage and Poundage, the customs duties (tax on imported goods) that made up a large portion of the King's annual income. Parliament now opted to re-evaluate these amounts annually, giving them more control over the King. James the 1ˢᵗ had resisted this and dealt with the problem by dissolving Parliament. Charles 1ˢᵗ did the same at first and later just ignored the annual re-evaluations.

However, Charles 1ˢᵗ was at war with France and Spain and this drained away a lot of money from him and he was forced to call upon Parliament (1629) to make new taxes for him. Parliament would not do this until he had signed the Petition of Rights that established conditions in which Charles had to submit to the will of Parliament. The conditions were as follows:

- The King could not establish martial law in England during times of peace;
- The King could not levy taxes without the consent of Parliament;
- The King could not arbitrarily imprison people;
- The King could not quarter soldiers in private homes.

After Charles got the taxes from Parliament in 1629, he then turned round and dissolved Parliament and broke the tenets of the Petition of Rights, since he believed in the Divine Rights of Kings Theory. Following a series of wars, both external and internal, which forced Charles to go once again to Parliament, terms were laid out which he had to agree to which ultimately made him the first constitutional monarch. Most important of these terms was that Charles had to agree to never dissolve a Parliament without the consent of the Parliament.

Following a series of events, Charles 1st stormed Parliament and then left London and went to Oxford and the English Civil War (1642) had begun. The North and West of England were on Charles 1st's side, along with most of the Nobles and country gentry. They were known as the Cavaliers. Charles created an illegal army (since he needed Parliament's consent).

The South and East of England were on Parliament's side and were known as the Roundheads, because of their haircuts. Parliament also raised an army. Because they didn't have the military might that Charles had they enlisted the help of the Scottish. They called their army the New Model Army and made its commander Oliver Cromwell. The New Model Army was composed mostly of Presbyterians. Parliament won the civil war and the Scots were paid off and sent back to Scotland. The Presbyterian Roundheads were not interested in imposing their religion on the country but only in having freedom to practice their religion.

Cromwell proposed that Parliament re-instate the bishops of the Church of England and also Charles 1st as a constitutional monarch, but allow for the toleration of other religions. The people of England could accept Charles 1st back as King but not religious tolerance. They also wanted the New Model Army dissolved. The New Model Army refused this order and a further civil war broke out in 1648. On one side were the Scottish (having been enlisted by Charles 1st) and the Royalists plus the Parliamentary Presbyterians. On the other was the New Model Army and the rest of Parliament.

In the Battle of Preston (1648) Cromwell and his New Model Army defeated Charles 1st. One of Cromwell's officers, Colonel Pride, destroyed the Presbyterian majority in Parliament by driving out 143 Presbyterians leaving behind 60. The new parliament constituted the 'Rump' Parliament which exercised power. They abolished the monarchy and the House of Lords in Parliament and executed Charles 1st after a public trial. They also created a republic called the 'Commonwealth' which was, in reality, a dictatorship by Cromwell. Cromwell also defeated Charles 2nd in Scotland who subsequently fled to France. Cromwell then went to Ireland and massacred many Irish Catholics causing an Irish rebellion.

Cromwell died in 1658 and was succeeded by his son Richard, who proved incapable of unifying the diverse religious groups and was overthrown by General George Monk of Scotland. Monk invited the remnants of the Rump Parliament to reconvene.

The Rump Parliament dissolved itself and created a new Parliament. The new Parliament began the restoration of the monarchy by choosing Charles 2nd as King of England.

Post Civil War

As we have seen, the period from the invasion of the Normans to the end of the Civil war was one of great ferment and huge strides, albeit amidst great bloodshed, were made in developing a constitution which ensured that the powers of monarchy were limited and the powers of the people were expressed through Parliament.

Post Civil war, in 1649, the Diggers, a small people's political reform movement published *The True Levellers Standard Advanced: or, the State of the Community opened and Presented to the Sons of Men*. This is another important document in the history of British constitutionalism, though different in one very important sense, in that it came from the people instead of the state. They are sometimes called the 'True levellers' to distinguish themselves from a larger political group called the Levellers which supported the Republicans during the Civil War. The ideas of the Diggers can be best understood through such philosophies as anarchism, libertarianism and religious communism.

Expansion of the Electoral Franchise
Between 1832 and 1989, numerous Acts of Parliament increased the number of people allowed to vote. Currently all people over 18 can vote. See the chapter on Electoral law.

The Reforms of New Labour
In Labour's first term (1997-2001) it introduced a large package of constitutional reforms. The most major were:

- The creation of a devolved Parliament in Scotland and assemblies in Wales and Northern Ireland, with their own direct elections.
- The creation of a devolved assembly in London and the associated post of a directly elected Mayor.
- The beginning of a process of reform of the House of Lords including the removal of all but 92 hereditary peers.
- The incorporation of the European Convention of Human Rights into UK law by passing the Human Rights Act 1998.
- The passing of the Freedom of Information Act 2000.
- The passing of the Political parties, Elections and Referendums Act 2000, creating the Electoral Commission to regulate elections and referendums and, to an extent, party spending.

With (potted) history as a background we can now turn to the nature and characteristics of the British Constitution as it now exists and also the role of political institutions and parties in its development.

Ch.2

The Nature of the Constitution

Whereas most countries have a constitution, a written document, laying down the main rules governing the main structure and functions of government, which regulates the relationship between people and government, Britain has an unwritten constitution.

The classification of constitutions

KC Wheare, in Modern Constitutions, 2nd edition (1966) identifies six ways of classifying constitutions.

Written and unwritten

Countries with a document or set of documents intentionally drafted to be the fundamental law of the country have a written constitution. A prime example of such a country is the United States. This constitution needs a special procedure to amend it. It follows that all organs of government must act in a way that is compatible to it. Courts have jurisdiction to amend or enforce the constitution. Countries that do not have a set of documents have an unwritten constitution. A prime example of a country with an unwritten constitution is the United Kingdom.

Flexible and rigid

Where no special process is required to amend a constitution it is called 'flexible'. Where a special process is required it is called 'rigid'.

Supreme or subordinate to the legislature

Chief Justice Marshall in the US Supreme Court decision in Marbury v Madison (1803) said that an act of legislature which is repugnant to the constitution is void. The constitution is therefore supreme and the legislature must act in a way that is consistent with the constitution. In countries with an unwritten constitution the legislature is supreme. It can make or unmake any law as it sees fit.

Although the constitution is not written, and is not a formal document as is, for example, the United States, it still forms the rules by which government and people interrelate and also provides a measure of legitimacy of government actions. These rules are expressed with differing degrees of formality in the form of statutory provisions, case law and conventions of the constitution.

Federal and unitary constitutions
In a federal constitution the governmental powers are divided between a central government, or federal government and state, regional or provincial governments. Each state, region or province has its own government. In a unitary state all governmental powers originate from the central or national government.

Constitutions based or not based on the separation of powers
It is almost impossible to find a state where there is a complete separation of powers. In such a hypothetical system the legislature, executive and judiciary should check each other.

Republican and monarchical constitutions
Where the head of state is a president a country may be called a republic. If a country has a hereditary head of state it may be called a monarchy.

The United Kingdom
In the case of Britain, there are, in comparison to other countries, very few positive statements regarding the powers and duties of the organs of government. Essentially, the British Constitution

historically, does not contain any declarations of the rights of individuals, in the form of a Bill of Rights. Rules relating to matters such as freedom of speech and assembly were traditionally derived from and had the same status as any other rule of law. That said, The Human Rights Act has had the effect of incorporating the European Convention on Human Rights into British law and giving individuals rights which can be directly enforced in the UK courts.

The British Constitution can be seen as a flexible constitution in that it does not have the rigidity of most written constitutions as Parliament can repeal any law with a simple majority. The absence of a written constitution has allowed considerable changes to be made informally without amendment of those legal rules which do exist. Thus the constitution can evolve gradually.

Unitary constitution

Because, as we shall see a little later, all legislative powers stem from Parliament we have a unitary as opposed to a federal constitution. Any legislation passed by Parliament can be subsequently repealed, through the doctrine of parliamentary sovereignty. This means that power can be taken back through this process. For example, this happened in 1972 when the Westminster Parliament re-imposed direct rule in Northern Ireland and again in 2000 when the Northern Ireland assembly was suspended after the IRA failed to decommission its weapons.

****

Ch.3

Sources of Constitutional Law

The sources of constitutional law in the United Kingdom are statutes and the common law. In Thoburn v Sunderland City Council (2003) Laws LJ said that the law should recognise a hierarchy of Acts of Parliament based on the distinction between 'ordinary' and 'constitutional' statutes. He went on to say that a constitutional statute:

(a) conditions the legal relationship between the citizen and the state in some general, overarching manner; or
(b) enlarges or diminishes the scope of fundamental human rights.

Laws LJ concluded that the special status of constitutional statutes follows the special status of constitutional rights.

Although the United Kingdom does not have a written constitution there are many Acts of Parliament that are relevant to constitutional law. As we have seen, through following the history of the development of the British constitution, The Magna Carta 1297, the Bill of Rights Act 1689, The Act of Settlement 1700, The Union With Scotland Act 1706, The Reform Acts which distributed and enlarged the franchise (Representation of the Peoples act 1832, 1867 and 1884), The Human Rights Act 1998, The Scotland Act 1998 and the Government of Wales Act 1998, and the European Communities Act 1972, taking this country into what is now the European Union, are all examples.

Conventions of the Constitution

It is not easy to understand the British Constitution simply by reference to case law. It is far more complex than that. For example, there is the role played by the monarch. The Queen must give Royal assent to all legislation. She appoints the Prime Minister and also has the power to dissolve Parliament. However, in practice the powers of the Monarch have been diminished and we have a constitutional monarch. The Queen acts on the advice of her Prime Minister. Such changes in the power of the monarchy have arisen as a result of the convention that the monarch should not become politically involved and should be neutral, favouring no political party. Essentially, formal rules have to be seen in the light of constitutional conventions which can both expand and modify the existing strict legal rules.

Constitutional Conventions-the nature of conventions

AV Dicey, in *Introduction to the Study of Law of the Constitution (1885)* distinguished between law and conventions. Laws are enforceable in the courts, conventions are not.

Conventions are rules of constitutional behaviour which are non-legal. They are considered to be binding upon those who operate the constitution but are not enforced by the courts or Parliament. They may be recognised by the courts as part of the constitutional background against which a particular decision is taken but will not be directly enforced.

Elaborating on this, Sir Ivor Jennings, in *Cabinet Government (1969)* said that constitutional conventions are outside the law and not recognized by it. However, he used the case of Watt v Kesteven County Council (1955) to claim that not all legal provisions confer directly enforceable rights on the individual. The Court of Appeal had to decide whether a local education authority was in breach of statutory duty because it had failed to provide education for pupils in accordance with the wishes of their parents as required by s76 of the Education Act 1944. Denning LJ held that the duty to make schools available could be enforced only by the minister and that s76 did not create a cause of action entitling an individual to a remedy in the civil courts.

Different categories of constitutional conventions

AV Dicey focussed on the purpose of law and the jurisdiction of the courts. He was aware that there are different classes of rules. Some conventions are as important as laws. As political rules they are obeyed to a greater or lesser degree. Maitland, in *The Constitutional History of England (1961)* also recognized that that such rules differ in stringency and definiteness. Munro, in *Studies in Constitutional law (1999)* agreed with Maitland. he concluded that it was sensible to have a two-class approach where it is clear that groups of uniform non-legal rules of a high degree of stringency and definiteness exist.

Examples of constitutional conventions
Royal assent

Every Bill which has passed the necessary parliamentary stages must receive the Royal Assent in order to become an Act of Parliament. The Parliament Acts 1911 and 1949 permit a bill to become an Act without the assent of the House of Lords. Certain procedures surrounding the Royal Assent are governed by the Royal Assent Act 1967. The reigning monarch is not legally bound to grant the royal assent.

Constitutional conventions

The monarch will grant the royal assent to a bill which has either been passed by the House of Commons and the House of Lords or has received the assent of the House of Commons under the Parliament Acts 1911 and 1949.

Appointment of the Prime Minister

At common law, under the Royal Prerogative, the Monarch has unlimited power to appoint ministers, including the Prime Minister.

Constitutional conventions

The Government must have the confidence of the majority in the House of Commons. This means that the Prime Minister is appointed from the membership of the House of Commons. The Prime Minster is normally the leader of the political party with a majority of seats in the House of Commons. If the party of which the Prime Minister is a member loses its majority in the House of Commons, he, and the other members of government will normally resign before the first meeting of the new Parliament.

Constitutional conventions and hung parliaments

A hung parliament arises when, following a general election, no party has an overall majority in the House of Commons. In his work, The 2010 General Election Outcome and the Formation of the Conservative-Liberal Democrat Coalition Government (2011) Public Law 30-55, Robert Blackburn identifies three constitutional conventions which apply to hung parliaments:

- the incumbent Prime Minister has the first opportunity to continue in office and form an administration.
- the second is that he is unable to do that (and resigns, or is defeated on the Address or in a no- confidence motion at the meeting of the new Parliament) then the leader of the opposition is appointed Prime Minster.

- thirdly, it is for the political parties to negotiate any inter-party agreement for government among themselves without royal involvement.

The appointment of ministers
Legal rules
There are no legal rules governing the appointment of ministers beyond the Royal Prerogative at common law and those contained in the House of Commons (Disqualification) Act 1975, which limits the number of ministers that may be appointed from the membership of the House of Commons to 95. Once they are appointed, statutes like the Parliamentary and other Pensions Act 1971 and the Ministerial and other Pensions and Salaries Act 1991 govern the payment of salaries and pensions.

Constitutional conventions
The constitutional conventions which govern the appointment of ministers are, firstly, that the Monarch appoints ministers upon the advice of the prime minister, and secondly that ministers are individually responsible to parliament.

The Cabinet
Legal rules
The Cabinet is recognized in statutes concerning ministerial salaries and pensions.

Constitutional conventions
The most important convention governing the cabinet is collective responsibility. This means that Cabinet does not voice dissent on government policy once a decision is taken. However, there have been departures in relation to this. In Attorney General v Jonathan Cape Ltd (1975) the Attorney General sought permanent injunctions restraining the publishers Jonathan Cape Ltd from

publishing the diaries or extracts from the diaries of former Cabinet Minister Richard Crossman. The diaries contained accounts of disagreements on matters of policy and details of discussions concerning the appointments of senior civil servants. The Attorney General argued that all cabinet papers, discussions and proceedings were confidential and the court should restrain any disclosure if the public interest in concealment outweighed the public interest in the right to free publication. The judge decided to refuse the injunctions. The contents of the first volume of the diaries were such that their publication, after the lapse of nearly ten years, could not inhibit free discussion in the existing Cabinet and would not, therefore, prejudice the maintenance of the doctrine of joint cabinet responsibility.

Constitutional conventions becoming law

A constitutional convention can become law by statute. In 2006, the Joint Committee on Conventions was set up to consider the practicality of codifying the key conventions on the relationship between the two Houses of Parliament which affect the consideration of legislation. An example of how a convention may become law by statute is the codification of the Ponsonby Rule by the Constitutional Reform and Governance Act 2010. The Ponsonby Rule was a constitutional convention that treaties which did not come into force on signature, but which instead came into force later when governments expressed their consent to be bound through a formal act such as ratification, had to be laid before both Houses of Parliament as a Command Paper for a minimum sitting period of 21 days subject to a resolution of either house of either house that it should not be ratified. The rule gave no legal effect to such a resolution. Section 20 (1) of the Constitutional Reform and Governance Act 2010 provides that a treaty cannot be ratified unless a Minister of the Crown has laid a published copy of it before

Parliament which has 21 sitting days to object to its ratification by resolution.

Other sources
European Union law
Through our membership of the European Union, community law is an integral part of our law. The primary sources of community law are the Treaties (the three founding Treaties and the Treaty of the European Union). The secondary sources are regulations, directives and decisions of the Council and the Commission and the European Court of Justice. The European Court of Human Rights plays an increasingly important role.

****

Ch.4

The Rule of Law

The absence of a formal written constitution in The United Kingdom has meant that there is no positive statement of the basic values governing state actions, no formal guidelines, as there is for example in the United States, which can be used as a measure of the legitimacy of government action. The concept of the rule of law has been used by lawyers and others in an attempt to provide such a measure. The rule of law is not a set of legal rules as such and is not directly enforceable by the courts and there is no legal sanction for behaviour that contravenes it. It is best thought of as a guiding principle.

Dicey's concept of the rule of law

For Dicey, there were three essential features of the rule of law:

a) "It means the absolute supremacy or predominance of regular law as opposed to the influence of arbitrary power and excludes the existence of arbitrariness, of prerogative or even wide discretionary authority on part of the Government.

b) It means equality before the law, or the equal subjection of all classes to the ordinary law of the land and administered by the ordinary courts.

c) It means that the constitution is the result of the ordinary law of the land...the rights of the individual are secured by and enmeshed in the common law and not by a constitutional document which can be suspended by the stroke of a pen".

The reflection of the Rule of law in English Law

Dicey emphasised that no one should be above the law and that the law should apply to officials of government and citizens alike. The British courts have always accepted the need for officials to point to the sources of their powers (Entick v Carrington 1765). Actions cannot be justified simply because they are official. No one can be detained without the proper legal authority. However, there are several notable breaches of this principle. An obvious example of a breach is the refusal of bail. The Anti-Terrorism, Crime and Security Act 2001 which allows the detention of suspected international terrorists by order of the Home Secretary is also a clear breach of the principle.

Privileges and immunities given to the Crown have decreased over the years The Crown Proceedings Act 1947 made it easier to sue the Crown, although immunities and privileges do remain, the personal immunity of the Sovereign from being sued, the privilege of free speech given to Members of Parliament and diplomatic immunity for example.

Dicey clearly felt that stronger protection was given to constitutional rights by the ordinary law of the land than by a written constitution.

The supremacy of Parliament

An important characteristic of the British constitution has been that Parliament, not the constitution, was the supreme legal authority. While, in the majority of states, the legislature is limited by the constitution in what it can and cannot do, Parliament is subject to no such limitations. British courts have had no power to declare laws passed by Parliament invalid.

Dicey's view of Parliamentary supremacy

- Parliament was competent to pass laws on any subject

- Its laws could regulate the activities of anyone, anywhere

- Parliament could not bind its successors as to the content, manner and form of subsequent legislation

- Laws passed by Parliament could not be challenged in courts.

Legal limitations on the scope of Parliament's powers

Dicey argued that there was no legal limitation on the scope of Parliament's power. Parliament legislates on matters affecting every aspect of our lives. It has legislated on matters regarding aliens, even with regard to activities outside British territory.

It has been argued that British membership of the EU imposes a legal (not only a political) limitation on Parliament. The 1967 White Paper (Cmnd.3301) on the legal and constitutional implications of Membership of the EC, stated that Parliament's freedom of action would be limited in that it would have to refrain from passing legislation inconsistent with community law and would be under an obligation in certain instances to legislate to give effect to our community obligations. The European Communities Act 1972, s2(1) gives present and future community law legal force in the UK and s.2(2) provides for the implementation of community law by means of secondary legislation, but the Act does not specifically prohibit Parliament from enacting conflicting legislation.

The power of Parliament to bind its successors

The courts have long accepted Dicey's view that Parliament has no power to bind its successors either as to the manner or the form of subsequent legislation. Each successive Parliament is deemed to be all-powerful and has the power to make or unmake law.

It was said in Godden v Hales (1686) that Parliament was entitled to ignore any provision in an earlier Act purporting to prevent the Act being repealed in the normal way. This was followed in the case of Ellen Street Estates Ltd v The Minister of Health (CA 1934) where the court found that it was impossible for Parliament to enact that, in a subsequent statute dealing with the same subject matter, there should be no implied repeal.

The European Communities Act 1972

Several grounds have been suggested for holding that this Act cannot be repealed:

a) That by joining the European Economic Community, a new order was created. Within that new order Parliament is no longer all powerful and cannot amend or repeal any statute by which that order was established.

b) That by assigning rights and powers to the community in accordance with the Treaty provisions, Member States have limited their sovereign rights in such a way as to make it withdraw unilaterally. There is no evidence to suggest that the British courts would accept this view. Lord Denning in Macarthy Ltd v Smith (CA 1979) clearly envisaged that Parliament could repeal the 1972 Act although it would have to be done expressly and not by implication. The political view is that a right to withdraw exists.

c) That, ultimately, the validity of legislation depends on the rules of recognition employed by judges. The present norm of validity recognises the latest statutory intention of Parliament. It has been suggested that this norm has altered and that the courts will recognise as valid only legislation which has been passed by both houses and given the royal assent, has not been repealed expressly or impliedly and which accords with our obligation under community law.

A limitation on the Doctrine of Implied Repeal

In the case Thoburn v Sunderland City Council (QB, 2001) Laws L.J. stated that the common law had come to recognise that there were certain fundamental constitutional rights and thus a hierarchy of Acts of Parliament, ordinary statutes and constitutional statutes. While ordinary statutes may be repealed by implication, the latter can only be repealed by express words on the face of the statute.

Laws passed by Parliament cannot be challenged in the courts

Traditionally, the British courts have refused to consider the validity of an Act of Parliament either on the ground that Parliament had no power to pass it or on the ground that the statute had been improperly passed.

Substantive validity

Until the seventeenth century the courts would declare Acts of Parliament void if they considered them to be contrary to natural law, repugnant to the law or impossible to be performed. In modern times any such challenge has been totally unsuccessful. In R v Jordan (1967) Jordan, who had been sentenced for offences under the Race Relations Act 1965, applied for a writ of habeas corpus claiming that he had been convicted under an invalid law. He alleged that the statute in question was invalid in that it conflicted with a fundamental principle of natural law, the right of free speech. He claimed that no Act of Parliament could take away this right.

The argument was rejected by the court which simply stated that it had no power to consider the validity of an Act of Parliament. This view was endorsed by the House of Lords in British Rail Board v Pickin (HL 1974).

In order to maintain Parliamentary supremacy the Human Rights Act does not give the courts any power to declare legislation invalid where it conflicts with the European Court of Human Rights but simply allows the court to make a declaration of incompatibility (s.4). The onus is then on Parliament to change the law if it wishes.

Procedural irregularity

Acts of Parliament have also been challenged on the ground that they have been improperly passed. In 1842 an Act of Parliament was challenged on this ground (Edinburgh and Dalkeith Railway v Wauchope (HL 1842). Lord Campbell, upholding the validity of the Act, refused to investigate the internal workings of Parliament saying that if the Act appears valid on the face of it, then it must be accepted by the courts. If due process has been followed then it is up to Parliament to investigate.

****

Ch.5

Administration of Government

The Executive
The executive is responsible for the initiation, formulation, direction and implementation of general government policy. Decisions are taken by the cabinet and implemented by the relevant government departments, each headed by a minister. Although historically these powers derived from the Crown, today the monarch plays no real part in the process of government. The expression 'the Crown' is a collective term which covers not only the monarch but the actions of the executive exercising the traditional powers of the monarch to govern the country.

The source of much real power is the legislative authority of Parliament expressed through Acts of Parliament. There remain, however, residual powers once exercised by the monarch, known as prerogative powers.

The Monarch
The British monarch is described as a constitutional monarch, Head of State, Commonwealth, Armed Forces. The monarch also provides a focus for national unity. She (currently) performs a number of constitutional functions, giving royal assent to legislation, opening the new Parliament, appointing the Prime Minister and a number of other senior appointments. In practice, however, the monarch has no real power as she acts on the advice of her Prime Minister. Only a few honours remain in the personal grant of the monarch.

Prime Ministers have a weekly audience with the Queen. She will receive foreign Heads of State and ambassadors and she is supplied with copies of all cabinet papers and minutes, important Foreign Office communications and also a summary of daily events in Parliament.

The powers and functions of the State

The state has three types of function: legislative; judicial and executive. The legislative function is exercised mainly through Parliament which has the power to make laws of general applicability and to grant other bodies the power to make delegated legislation under authority of an Act of Parliament. Originally, the monarch had the power to make laws by means of royal proclamation. A residue of this power is to make orders in council.

The state also has the authority to determine disputes which arise out of the operation of its laws. Such disputes are allocated to tribunals or government ministers or courts.

The state has various executive functions. It must initiate, formulate and direct general policy. That policy must then be put into operation, monitored and regulated. Responsibility for this lies with the government of the country.

The doctrine of the separation of powers

Many writers and political thinkers, going back to Aristotle, have been concerned that if legislative, executive and judicial functions are concentrated in the same person or body this would lead to abuse of power. They have argued that power should be distributed to avoid abuse. One way of achieving this is by the doctrine of separation of powers. Each body would then be strong enough to counterbalance the others. There has never been a strict separation of powers in this country. Unlike the United States, the Prime

Minister and Cabinet are drawn from Parliament. Although Parliament is the main legislative organ, the courts and the executive both have legislative responsibilities. Government ministers have legislative, executive and judicial functions.

The doctrine of separation of powers is of particular value in that it helps to maintain the independence of the judiciary.

Prerogative power

The powers of the state must be exercised in accordance with the law by virtue of authority granted by the law. In modern times, this authority is generally granted by statute but certain powers, rights and immunities appertaining to the Crown still have their origins in the common law. These, originally exercised by the monarch personally, are known as prerogative powers.

The prerogative is a residual power and will be superseded by statute. Where the statutory provision deals with the same area, the prerogative may be extinguished either expressly or by implication. (See Attorney General v De Keyser's Royal Hotel (HL 1920).

Prerogatives may relate to the legislative, executive or judicial functions of government. Examples of prerogatives still in existence include:

- The administration of overseas territories by means of orders in council

- Authority to make treaties

- The recognition of foreign states

- Declarations of war and peace

- The disposition and control of the armed forces

- Power to take action in an emergency

- The prerogative of mercy

- The power to stop criminal prosecutions

- The granting of the royal assent to legislation

- The summoning and dissolution of Parliament

- Granting of honours.

Prerogative also includes the immunities of the Crown such as the monarch's immunity from prosecution.

In the past, the courts were reluctant to interfere with prerogative powers. In Laker Airways v Department of Trade (HC 1976) the court indicated that while it would determine the existence and the scope of prerogative power it would not review the propriety or adequacy of the grounds on which it had been exercised. However, in Council for Civil Service Unions v Minister of the Civil Service (HL 1984) the House of Lords recognised the possibility of reviewing the exercise of prerogative power on the same grounds as power granted under statutory provisions. It rationalised this by saying that nowadays the question of whether a power was authorised by statute or prerogative was largely a matter of historical accident.

The Cabinet and the Prime Minister

All major government decisions are taken by the Cabinet committee of senior government ministers. The Cabinet determines the policies to be submitted to Parliament, to determine the content and priorities of legislative proposals and to ensure that the relevant polices are carried out. By convention, all members of the Cabinet are collectively responsible for decisions taken. While the matter is under discussion ministers can air their views but once the matter is decided then all members of the Government inside and outside of the Cabinet must support it. If they are unable to do this then they must resign. High profile resignations have been Michael Heseltine over the Westland affair and Robin Cook over Iraq.

As with the Cabinet itself, the office of Prime Minister is one which is barely recognised in the law. It is true to say that this century has seen a steady increase in the powers of the Prime Minister, who is now in a very strong position.

a) As leader of the party in power, he has been chosen by the electorate, has control over the party machinery and can (usually) rely on the strength of party unity to maintain his position.

b) As chairman of the Cabinet, he can to a large extent determine the nature of discussions within the Cabinet. No votes are customarily taken. Rather the Prime Minister will sum up the sense of the meeting. Matters can be referred to sub-committees and the agenda manipulated to ensure the desired result.

c) As ultimate head of the civil service, the Prime Minister has powers over senior appointments and access to all information.

d) The Cabinet Office, although technically providing a service for all members of the Cabinet, has grown into the Prime Minister's special source of assistance and information. This greatly strengthens the Prime Minister's ability to argue against proposals put forward by departmental ministers who are forced to rely almost entirely on the briefs prepared for them by their departmental civil servants. This has been supplemented in recent years by a substantial increase in so-called 'special advisors'.

e) The Prime Minster is the source of much patronage. He will appoint or dismiss government ministers and have at his disposal a wide selection of public appointments, honours and so on.

Government ministers and departments

The various tasks undertaken by Central Government are executed by the various government departments such as the Foreign Office and the Treasury. A government minister will head these departments assisted by junior ministers. Each Minister has a Parliamentary Private Secretary. These people will usually be MP's from either the House of Commons or the House of Lords. Although there is no legal limit on the number of ministers there is a limit in the number who can sit and vote in the House of Commons, currently 95 and a limit to the number of ministerial salaries that can be paid.

Departments are staffed by professional civil servants each one headed by a Permanent Secretary. Civil servants will serve whatever government is in power notwithstanding whether they agree with the government or not.

Ministerial responsibility

Ministers are responsible to Parliament for the conduct of their departments. They may be legally responsible for the acts and omissions of their department and Government Agencies connected to them. Parliament has the right to question the minister on any aspect of the work of the department, even regarding events which took place prior to the minister taking office. The Ministerial Code

(1997) reminds ministers of their duty to give accurate and truthful information to Parliament and be truthful and open in accordance with the Code of Practice on Access to Government Information.

Ministers who feel personally to blame for a serious breach will normally resign their post. For example, Lord Carrington as Foreign Secretary following the invasion of the Falkland Islands and, famously, John Profumo who was involved in a personal scandal.

The availability of personal information

The traditional attitude of government has been that information should remain secret unless the government chooses to make it available. The argument has been that disclosure is not in the public interest. The government will go to some lengths to suppress information, as was shown when it tried to suppress the memoirs of ex-government agent Peter Wright (spycatcher) although in the end it was seen not to be of any great importance.

Courts have also protected the secrecy of Cabinet discussions by granting injunctions and refusing applications for discovery of documents. In the case Attorney General v Jonathan Cape Limited (HC 1976) the court held that it had the power to restrain publication of material relating to such discussions, although the power was not then exercised.

The Public Records Acts

The Public Records Acts 1958-1967 protected cabinet documents and other government papers for 30 years, unless the government chose to make them available. The period could be extended if continued secrecy was deemed to be in the public interest. The Freedom of Information Act 2000 replaces the largely discretionary regime for access to public records with a new statutory regime and provides enhanced access to records more than 30 years old.

The Official Secrets Acts 1911-89

The climate of secrecy was encouraged and supported by the Official Secrets Acts 1911-20, which were used not simply to prevent disclosure of security information but to prevent the disclosure of all information which government chose to keep secret whether or not there were national security implications. The emphasis of the very first Act in 1889 was to prevent spying. The 1911 Act strengthened this. Section 1 of the Act covers all forms of spying making it an offence if any person, for purposes prejudicial to the interests of the state:

a) Approaches, infects...enters any prohibited place or

b) Makes any sketches, plans models or notes which may be useful to the enemy

c) Obtains or communicates to any other person any information...calculated or intended to be, or which might be useful to the enemy.

In the case Chandler v DPP (HL 1964) members of a group supporting nuclear disarmament were convicted under s.1 following an incident where they entered an RAF base and attempted to obstruct its use. This sabotage was held to fall within the conduct prohibited by s.1. The House of Lords held that the question whether the conduct was prejudicial to the interests of the state was for the court and not for the jury.

Section 2 of the 1920 Act provided that communicating with a foreign agent is evidence of obtaining or attempting to obtain information calculated or intended to be useful to an enemy contrary to s.1 of the Act. Overall the Official Secrets Acts go far beyond spying making it an offence to disclose or reveal official information.

The Official Secrets Act 1989, which repealed s.2 of the 1920 Act, is designed to protect more limited classes of official information. Section 1(1) makes it an offence for any member or former member of the security and intelligence services to disclose information relating to, or in support of those services. Where the disclosure is by a Crown servant or contractor, only those disclosures which are damaging to the public interest are criminalised. No such public interest defence is available to members of the security services charged under s.1(1) as in the case R v Shayler (HL 2001).

The Defence Advisory Notice System

In addition to the restrictions arising out of the Official Secrets Acts, the media is further restricted in what it can publish by a system of self-censorship known as the Defence Advisory Notice System. A lot of material used by journalists is obtained from official sources 'off the record'. However, because of official secrets legislation and the effect of laws on breach of confidence and contempt, the use of such information may constitute a breach of the law. Editors of various media will require some kind of guidance as to whether action may be likely following a particular disclosure. This informal guidance is given by the Defence, Press and Broadcasting Advisory Committee which is made up of civil servants and representatives of the media. It issues 'Defence Advisory' Notices advising that those matters listed should not be published as they are required to remain secret for security reasons. Categories presently covered include information about nuclear weapons installations and highly classified military information along with information about the intelligence services.

Freedom of information

The Freedom of Information Act 2000 regulates the availability of information and ensures that information about the workings of government is freely available. The 2000 Act is the culmination of many years of lobbying and the Act introduced a general right of access to information held by a wide range of public authorities listed in s.1 of the Act such as local and national government departments, schools universities and hospitals, subject to certain conditions and exemptions. These exemptions, laid out in Pt 11 of the Act include security information, defence matters criminal proceedings and information whose disclosure is likely to prejudice the country's economic interests.

****

Ch.6

The Role of Parliament

In the previous chapter, we saw how the government of the United Kingdom is administrated, discussing the role of the executive and ministerial responsibility. In this chapter, we examine more closely the workings of Parliament.

The composition of Parliament
Parliament consists of three elements:
a) The Monarch. The Monarch gives the royal assent to legislation. As we have seen the role is now essentially formal.

b) The House of Lords.

c) The House of Commons.

The House of Lords
The House of Lords is currently a non-elected chamber. In 2016, it consists of:

The Lords Temporal:
a) 92 Hereditary Peers and Peeresses in their own right. The House of Lords Act 1999 removed the right of all other Hereditary Peers to sit and vote. Those remaining were elected by their peers.

b) Life Peers appointed under the Life Peerages Act 1958 (458).

c) Lords of Appeal in Ordinary.

The Lords Spiritual-26 Bishops of the Church of England comprising the Archbishops of Canterbury and York, the Bishops of London, Durham and Winchester and 21 other bishops in order of seniority of appointment. They sit only as long as they hold Episcopal office.

If a person is an alien, under 21, un-discharged bankrupt, a person convicted of treason or a member expelled by the house unless pardoned then they are disqualified from the House of Lords.

The House of Lords Reform Act 2014 received the Royal Assent in 2014.[38] Under the new law:

- All peers can retire or resign from the chamber (prior to this only hereditary peers could disclaim their peerages).
- Peers can be disqualified for non-attendance.
- Peers can be removed for receiving prison sentences of a year or more.[38]

The House of Commons

There are a total of 650 (2016) Members of Parliament elected on a constituency basis by those entitled to vote by virtue of the Representation of People's Acts 1983-2000. All Commonwealth citizens and citizens of Northern Ireland are entitled to vote if they are 18 and registered to vote. Those compulsorily detained under the Mental Health Acts are not eligible to vote as are persons convicted of certain corrupt or illegal practices at elections. Prisoners have traditionally been disenfranchised although in the case Hirst v UK (ECHR 2004) it was held that a blanket ban on all prisoners irrespective of the offence or length of sentence was in breach of the European Convention on Human Rights. The 2000 Act allows people of no fixed abode to register by allowing them to make a declaration of a local connection.

Disqualification for membership of the House of Commons

a) Aliens.

b) Persons under 21.

c) Persons of unsound mind.

d) Bankrupts until discharged.

e) Persons guilty of corrupt or illegal practices at elections.

f) Persons guilty of treason until sentence completed or pardon granted. A person convicted of an offence and sentenced to more than one year. This covers imprisonment in the UK or Republic of Ireland.

g) Those disqualified under the House of Commons Disqualification Act 1975 as 'holding an office or place of profit under the Crown'.

Devolution of Government

The Scotland Act 1998

This Act established a Scottish Parliament in Edinburgh. There are 129 members, 73 of whom are elected under a simple majority system and the remainder by proportional representation using the additional member system. Section 28 authorises the parliament to make laws known as the Acts of the Scottish Parliament. The Scottish Parliaments legislative powers are limited by s.29 which reserves certain matters for the Westminster Parliament. These are listed in Sch. 5 and include foreign affairs, defence of the realm and many other financial and economic matters. Under s.29 (20(d)) a provision is outside the competence of the Parliament if it is incompatible with rights under the European Convention on Human Rights or with Community Law. The Act does not preclude the Westminster Parliament from legislating for Scotland. The Act created a Scottish Executive consisting of a First Minister and Ministers drawn from the Scottish Parliament.

Government of Wales Act 1998

This Act set up the National Assembly for Wales. This does not have the legislative powers of the Scottish Parliament but carries out administrative functions formerly exercised by the Secretary of State for Wales. Such powers are transferred to the Assembly by means of Orders in Council and include agriculture, education and economic development. There are no powers to change rates of taxation.

As with the Scottish Parliament the members are elected by a mixed system.

The Northern Ireland Act 1998

Following the Good Friday Agreement in 1998, an elected Assembly was established consisting of 108 members representing 18 constituencies elected by means of the single transferable vote system. Section 1 of the Act declares that Northern Ireland in its entirety remains part of the United Kingdom and shall not cease to be so without the consent of the majority of the people of Northern Ireland. The Assembly has powers to make laws known as Acts. As with Scotland certain matters are reserved for Westminster Parliament.

The work of Parliament
The passage of legislation

At the beginning of each parliamentary session, the Monarch opens Parliament with a speech from the throne which outlines the Governments main proposals for the session. The Cabinet decides on a timetable for introduction of legislation.

The preparation of legislation is a lengthy process. The content and policy of the original Bill must be approved by the relevant Cabinet Committee and then by full Cabinet. Reform may sometimes be preceded by Green or White papers allowing consultation in

Parliament. Consultation will also take place with various interest groups who will be directly affected by the legislation. By the end of this pre-legislative stage the content of the bill is effectively settled although further negotiations will continue throughout the passage to Parliament. Parliamentary draftsmen will draft the bill at the outset, officially known as the Parliamentary Counsel to the Treasury.

Joint Committee on Human Rights

All public Bills are now examined by the Joint Committee on Human Rights to determine whether it is convention compliant. The Joint Committee reports back to both Houses. The Government must, by the second reading, indicate whether the Bill is compatible with the convention. The Human Rights Act does not prevent Parliament passing legislation which conflicts with our obligations under the ECHR but any non-compliance must be clearly indicated.

The following is the procedure for the passing of a Public Bill introduced by the Government into the House of Commons:

1. First reading

The title of the Bill is read out then an order is made for the Bill to be published and a date fixed for the second reading.

2. Second reading

The principles of the Bill are discussed on the floor of the House.

3. Committee stage

A detailed clause-by-clause analysis of the Bill by a standing committee of between 16-50 MP's. Detailed amendments are considered.

4. Report stage

The Bill is reported back to the whole house as amended. Further amendments can be made at this stage.

5. Third reading

The whole house considers the principles behind the legislation. Only verbal amendments can be made and any debate must be supported by at least six members.

Once a Bill has passed the Commons stage it goes up to the House of Lords where the same stage process is repeated, except that the Committee stage is taken on the floor of the House. If the Bill is amended by the House of Lords, these amendments must be considered by the Commons. If the amendments are rejected by the Commons, the Lords must decide whether to carry on, or persist with these. If no agreement is reached by the end of the session, the Bill will fail. The Government must then decide whether or not to reintroduce the Bill in the next session and invoke the provisions of the Parliament Acts of 1911-49.

Once the Bill is passed by both Houses, it receives the Royal Assent. This is purely formal. There are variations to the above procedure in certain cases, as below:

1. Bills may start life in either House. The Government must try to arrange its business to ensure that the Commons does not have all its work at the beginning of the session and the House of Lords has all its work at the end. As the House of Commons has sole responsibility for financial matters, it has to carry the burden of the work on financial Bills.
2. Some Bills have their Second Reading stage in Committee. This is on the motion of a minister but can be prevented if 20 members object. This procedure was introduced in an

attempt to save time on the floor of the House and is used for unopposed and non-controversial legislation. If the Second Reading is in Committee then the report stage will also be in Committee.

3. Some Bills have their committee stage on the floor in the House of Commons. This procedure can be used for:

    (a) non-controversial Bills where the committee stage would be purely formal
    (b) Bills of major constitutional importance where all members wish to be involved at every stage;
    (c) Bills passed in an emergency;
    (d) Major clauses of finance Bills.

Parliamentary scrutiny-how effective is it?

Many see that the present procedure for the passage of legislation does not provide effective scrutiny and that parliament quite simply legitimises that which the Government has decreed. There are a number of factors that indicate that scrutiny is ineffective.

1. The Government has the majority in Commons and can normally force its measures through relying on such factors as the "whip system" and party loyalty.
2. The Government has control over the parliamentary timetable and can curtail discussions and bring matters to a vote by use of various procedural devices such as the "closure". If a voluntary timetable cannot be agreed then the Government can "guillotine" proceedings.
3. As legislation has increased in complexity over the years, MP's may lack the experience to adequately question the Bill.
4. The power of the House of Lords to amend legislation is limited by the Parliament Acts 1911-49.

Notwithstanding the above perceived limitations, Bills are normally considerably amended during their passage through Parliament. New clauses may be added to a Bill and concessions will be made. Parliamentary scrutiny is still important as:

(a) It ensures the measure is publicised allowing opinion outside parliament to make itself known.
(b) The Government may be able to ignore the opposition but it cannot afford to ignore its own supporters.
(c) Establishment of Departmental Select Committees has increased the flow of independent information to MP's and increased specialist knowledge amongst backbenchers to enable them to scrutinise legislation more effectively.
(d) Party ties are less strong in committee and defeats do occur for the Government.
(e) If the House of Lords exercises its power of delay it ensures maximum publicity for the measure in question. Amendments are sometimes accepted by the Government against its better judgement to prevent disruption of the Parliamentary timetable.

Private Member's Bills

Backbenchers can introduce Bills in the following circumstances:

1. By being successful in the Ballot.
2. Under the Ten-Minute rule.
3. Under Standing Order 57.

On average 10-12 Private Member's Bills become law each session. These are mainly ballot Bills.

Ballot Bills

At a ballot at the beginning of each session 20 names are drawn out of a hat by the Deputy Speaker. Those members, in order, have the opportunity to introduce the Bills before the House. Six Fridays are set aside in each session for the passage of such Bills although the Government can give extra time to those Bills it supports to ensure success.

The subjects chosen are wide ranging. The only restriction is that the main purpose of the Bill must not be public expenditure. If some incidental expenditure is involved the member must persuade the minister to move a financial resolution.

The procedure is identical to that of any other public Bill. Responsibility for drafting the Bill is given to the member although assistance can be given if there is a chance of the Bill becoming law.

Ten-Minute Rule Bills

Under Standing Order 23 on Tuesdays and Wednesdays, one member, selected by the Speaker on a first come first served basis, has ten minutes in which to outline his proposal for legislation. It is very unlikely that legislation will result from this. The main purpose of this procedure is not to invite legislation but to generate publicity for a particular issue or to test the water to see if there is support for legislation in the future. Even if a "Bill" succeeds at this stage there is no time allocated for further stages and so, unless the Government gives up some of its time, the Bill will not proceed further.

Standing Order 57

Under the above, a member may present a Bill without obtaining leave from the House. This allows a member to take advantage of any gap in the Parliamentary timetable and present a measure, although gaps are rare.

Delegated legislation

Not all legislation is made directly by Parliament. Government ministers, local authorities and other public bodies have been given the power by statute to make subordinate legislation. This may be in the form of statutory instruments and orders, byelaws, regulations and orders in council.

The most important type of delegated legislation made by a minister is a statutory instrument. This is defined and regulated by the Statutory Instruments Act 1946. Delegated legislation made by a minister acting under statutory authority which does not fall within this definition, is known as a statutory order.

Uses of delegated legislation

Delegated legislation is used mainly to add detail to primary legislation which may lay down the general principles although matters of considerable importance are sometimes dealt with in this way. The use of delegated legislation saves parliamentary time as Parliament can concentrate on the principles and ignore the details which can be worked out elsewhere. Delegated legislation also allows a certain flexibility in the law. For example, it enables the minister to bring sections of an Act into effect as and when required.

Control over delegated legislation
The enabling Act.

The law-making power which Parliament intends to delegate should be expressed in clear and unambiguous language. The grant of wide discretionary powers makes it difficult to control the exercise of these powers by means of the doctrine of *ultra vires*. The enabling Act also determines the form in which the power is to be exercised. Greater control will be achieved by providing that the power is to be exercised by way of statutory instrument. It will then be regulated by the Statutory Instruments Act 1946 and will, if laid before Parliament be subject to the scrutiny of the joint Committee on Delegated Legislation.

Laying before Parliament

The enabling Act can provide that the instrument can be laid before either or both Houses of Parliament. Various types of laying procedures are used:

(a) Greatest control is achieved by making the order subject to an affirmative resolution. This means the instrument will not come into effect until approved by Parliament in accordance with the laying requirement. Such instruments are automatically referred to a standing committee unless the House orders otherwise but the Government will have a majority in the committee and can normally force its measures through.

(b) Where an order is subject to a negative resolution it must be laid before Parliament (usually for 40 days) during which time a member can move a prayer to annul it. The order may come into effect as soon as it is signed by a relevant minister. If annulled it will simply cease being law.

(c) Other forms of laying procedure are laying for information only and laying in draft.

Section 4 of the Statutory Instruments Act 1946 says that where a statutory instrument is required to be laid before Parliament then it shall be laid before the instrument comes into operation. This is subject to the proviso that where it is essential that an instrument comes into effect immediately, it can be brought into effect before it is laid, but that the Speaker and / or Lord Chancellor shall be informed of this and the reason for it.

Publication

Not all delegated legislation needs to be published, which can undermine the process of adequate scrutiny. In the case of statutory orders, any specific requirements as to publication must be stated in the enabling Act. Statutory instruments are regulated by s.2 of the Act and must be sent to the Queen's printer numbered and out on sale. Some statutory instruments are exempt from this requirement by the Statutory Instruments Regulations 1947. This exempts instruments of a local or temporary nature, bulky Schedules and instruments which, in the opinion of the minister, it is not in the public interest to publish.

Scrutiny by Parliamentary Committee

The Joint Committee on Statutory Instruments, which comprises seven members from each House plus a chairman drawn from the opposition benches in the Commons, can examine all general statutory instruments and all other statutory orders subject to the affirmative procedure or special procedure orders. It is not concerned with the merits of the instruments but rather with whether the attention of the House should be drawn to the legislation in that it:

(a) imposes a tax or a fee on the public or a charge on the public revenue;

(b) is made pursuant of an enactment containing specific provisions excluding it from a challenge in the courts;

(c) purports to have retrospective effect when there is no express authority in the enabling statute;

(d) has been unduly delayed in publication or laying before Parliament;

(e) has come into operation before being laid before Parliament and there has been unjustifiable delay in informing the speaker;

(f) is of doubtful *vires* or makes some unusual or unexpected use of the powers conferred by the enabling statute;

(g) calls for any special reason of form or content, for elucidation;

(h) is defective in its drafting.

Scrutiny by the courts

The courts may be asked to consider whether delegated legislation is *ultra vires* the enabling Act. In interpreting the scope of the power to make delegated legislation, the courts will apply certain presumptions, e.g. that there is no power to impose a tax unless stated expressly.

Debates

The opposition parties have 20 days in each session in which they can select the topic for debate. Emergency Debates are allowed at the discretion of the Speaker under standing order 24 if he considers that an application relates to a "specific and important matter that should have urgent consideration." The application must be supported by 40 members.

Parliamentary questions

Ministers are questioned in the House on a rota basis for 45 or 55 minutes on Mondays to Thursdays. The Prime Minister faces questions only once a week on a Wednesdays. Members can give no more than 10 days notice of a question and the questions are listed in the order in which they are tabled.

Written answers to questions

Questions not dealt with on the floor of the House are answered in writing by the minister and the answers published in Hansard. In addition, questions may be put down for written answer. Such questions are designed:

(a) to obtain factual information;
(b) to make up matters on behalf of constituents.

One basic defect in these methods of scrutiny is that MP's must know the right questions to ask. As Government becomes more complex, it becomes increasingly difficult for MP's to have sufficient specialist knowledge to identify the key areas for investigation.

Parliamentary select committees

A more effective method of scrutiny is by Parliamentary select committees comprised of groups of MP's. Currently there are 16 such committees shadowing the various departments of state, including Constitutional affairs, Education and Skills and Culture, Media and Sport.

Membership of the committees normally consists of 11 MP's their membership reflecting a balance of the House. The chairmanships are shared between the main parties, the Government retaining some of the most sensitive, e.g. defence for itself. The committee members are appointed by the Committee of Selection.

Terms of reference

The terms of reference is stated as follows "To provide continuous and systematic scrutiny of the activities of the public services and to base that scrutiny on the subject areas within the responsibility of the individual Government Departments".

Specifically the committees have the following functions:

(a) To examine departmental estimates, to examine the policy objectives underlying these and consider whether the expenditure incurred would achieve these objectives in an economical manner.

(b) To examine all aspects of administration and policy relating to the department.
(c) To undertake special duties of areas of importance within the ambit of the department.
(d) To have a limited function in the examination of delegated legislation and European Secondary Legislation.

Committees also measure departmental performance against a number of targets.

Powers of committees
The committees are empowered to take evidence from ministers, civil servants and outside experts and to call for necessary papers and evidence. They will question regulators and the chairs of various executive agencies.

Financial control
Parliament has control over taxation and expenditure, although final decisions are made by the government. The Chancellor of the Exchequer now usually combines the statement on public expenditure with the budget speech. Taxes imposed annually must be authorised by the Finance Act. Authority for levying taxation in the interim period is given by the Provisional Collection of Taxes Act 1968, a resolution of the House of Commons being insufficient authority. (see Bowles v Bank of England (1913)).

The Comptroller and Auditor General, appointed by the Crown on a resolution of the House of Commons by virtue of s.1 (1) of the National Audit Act 1983 has two major functions:

a) to ensure that all money paid out of the government accounts has been properly authorised and is properly applied; and
b) to examine the accounts of the various government departments.

There will then be a report to the public accounts committee who will examine a selection of the reports. The National Audit Office is also responsible for auditing the accounts of a wide range of bodies dependent on funds from central government, such as the NHS and Universities.

Parliamentary privilege

Members of Parliament and Parliament as a whole have certain privileges to enable them to carry out their functions correctly. One of these privileges, in fact the main privilege is that of freedom of speech.

MP's have **absolute** privilege with regards to what they say during Parliamentary proceedings. This arises under the Bill of Rights Act, Article 9. This protects against defamation and also against criminal charges. In one notable case, Church of Scientology v Johnson Smith (HC 1972) an attempt was made to sue an MP claiming that he had slandered the Church of Scientology and its members. In order to succeed in this case it had to be shown that the MP had spoken with malice. It was attempted to prove this by using words spoken in parliament. This was not upheld as the words were absolutely privileged.

However, it does not always follow that everything that is said and done within the confines of the chamber during a debate is covered by Parliamentary privilege, not everything forms part of proceedings in Parliament. It would not, for example, cover private conversations between Members of Parliament. There have been problems relating to letters written by MP's to Ministers in the course of their duties. This question arose in both the Sandys case (1938) and Strauss (1958)

Duncan Sandys 1938

In the *Duncan Sandys* case (1938-39) the House had agreed with the Select Committee on the Official Secrets Acts that the working definition of 'proceedings' should be extended to communications between one Member and another or between a Member and a Minister so closely related to some matter pending in or expected to be brought before the House that they form part of the business of the House.

Mr Sandys, the Conservative Member for Norwood, was also a serving officer in the Territorial Army. He had sent a written draft of parliamentary question to the Secretary of State for War, which incorporated highly sensitive and detailed information about the deficiencies of anti-aircraft provision in London. Subsequently the Attorney General informed Mr Sandys that he had a legal obligation to reveal the source of his information, or face the consequences under the Official Secrets Act. Although the Attorney General later assured Mr Sandys that he personally would not face prosecution, Mr Sandys raised the issue as a matter of privilege, which was referred to an ad hoc Select Committee.

In its Report, the Select Committee on the Official Secrets Act referred to matters 'so closely related to some matter pending in, or expected to be brought before, the House, that though they do not take place in the chamber or a committee room they form part of the business of the House, as, for example, where a member sends to a Minister the draft of a question he is thinking of putting down or shows it to another member with a view to obtaining advice as to the propriety of putting it down or as to the manner in which it should be framed.' The Attorney-General told the Select Committee that, should such a case come before the courts, he could not but think that they would give a broad construction to the term 'proceeding in parliament' having regard to the great

61

fundamental purpose which the privilege of freedom of speech served, and that he could 'see a possible construction of "proceedings" which would extend to matters outside the precincts if they were related to what is to happen in the House'.

George Strauss 1958

In the *Strauss* case (1958), the House of Commons decided not to endorse the view of the Committee of Privileges that a letter written by a Member of the House of Commons to a Minister concerning the day-to-day administration of a nationalised industry was a proceeding in Parliament.

Speaking in the debate on the *Strauss* case, the Leader of the House (R. A. Butler) expressed the opinion that the 1939 decision in the *Sandys* case had marked the "high tide" of Parliamentary privilege. The *Strauss* case also dealt with communications between a Member and a Minister, but the connection to parliamentary proceedings was not as clear as in the *Sandys* case. George Strauss, the Member for Vauxhall, had written to the Paymaster General, Reginald Maudling (Conservative) criticising the scrap metal dealings of the London Electricity Board as "a scandal" open to "strong suspicion" and alleging that there had been "day to day maladministration' .... "in the nature of a public scandal".

Mr Strauss declared in his letter to the Minister that he had an indirect personal financial interest, in that a subsidiary of his firm were scrap metal merchants who shared the view of the LEB's behaviour held by the National Association of Non-Ferrous Scrap Metal Merchants. Under the rules applying to parliamentary questions at the time, Mr Strauss would have been unable to raise in a parliamentary question such a matter of day-to-day administration by a nationalised industry. The Minister passed Mr Strauss's letter on to the LEB, who threatened to sue Mr Strauss for defamation.

Mr Strauss's complaint of a breach of privilege was referred to the Committee of Privileges.

The Committee of Privileges "adopted and followed" the reasoning of the Select Committee in the *Duncan Sandys* case by concluding that Mr Strauss in writing to the Paymaster General directing his attention to matters of administration in a nationalised industry was conducting or engaged in a "proceeding in Parliament" and that in so doing he was protected by Article 9 of the Bill of Rights.

But a motion to approve the Committee's Reports on the case was debated on 8 July 1958. Herbert Morrison successfully moved an amendment "to leave out from "House" to the end of the Question and to add instead thereof: "does not consider that Mr. Strauss's letter of the 8th February, 1957, was 'a proceeding in Parliament' and is of opinion therefore that the letters from the Chairman of the London Electricity Board and the Board's Solicitors constituted no breach of Privilege".

Joint Committee on the Publication of Proceedings in Parliament 1970

The Joint Committee on the Publication of Proceedings in Parliament recommended that "proceedings in Parliament" should be defined by statute, and offered the following definition (Second Report, Session 1969–70, HL 109/ HC 261, paragraph 27)—

"(1) For the purpose of the defence of absolute privilege in an action or prosecution for defamation the expression 'proceedings in Parliament' shall without prejudice to the generality thereof include:

a) all things said done or written by a Member or by any officer of either House of Parliament or by any person ordered or authorised to attend before such House, in or in the presence of such House and in the course of a sitting of such House, and for the purpose of the business being or about to be transacted, wherever such sitting may be held and whether or not it be held in the presence of strangers to such House: provided that for the purpose aforesaid the expression 'House' shall be deemed to include any Committee sub-Committee or other group or body of members or members and officers of either House of Parliament appointed by or with the authority of such House for the purpose of carrying out any of the functions of or of representing such House; and

b) all things said done or written between Members or between Members and officers of either House of Parliament or between Members and Ministers of the Crown for the purpose of enabling any Member or any such officer to carry out his functions as such provided that publication thereof be no wider than is reasonably necessary for that purpose."

Qualified privilege

An MP may rely on the defence of qualified privilege in regard to words spoken in the course of his duty as an MP. This means that he or she is protected against any act of defamation provided that he speaks in good faith and without malice (see Beach v Freeson (HC 1972)) and provided that there is a common interest between the parties. Some MP's, in recent years, have made good use of this particular privilege to make defamatory allegations. Following the case of Prebble v Television New Zealand Ltd (1995) the High Court halted a libel action by Neil Hamilton MP against the Guardian Newspaper on the basis that much of the evidence could not be explored as it related to "Proceedings in parliament".

In October 1994, *The Guardian* accused two Members of Parliament, Mr Hamilton and Mr Tim Smith, of having accepted cash sums from Mr Mohamed Al Fayed for parliamentary services, in particular asking a large number of parliamentary questions over a period of months or years in Mr Al Fayed's interest, and of having failed to declare the payments in the Register of Members' Interests. Mr Greer, a well known parliamentary lobbyist, was alleged to have been the conduit for some of the payments, both to Mr Hamilton and to Mr Smith. *The Guardian's* source was, of course Mr Al Fayed, and his credibility, and any corroboration which could be obtained for his evidence, would have been the main issue at the trial. Immediately after the publication of the Guardian's story, Mr Smith resigned his ministerial office. In his letter of resignation to the Prime Minister, he admitted having accepted payments from Mr Al Fayed, which he had not declared. Mr Smith did not sue *The Guardian,* and thereafter steadfastly declined to elaborate on his letter to the Prime Minister, until the Parliamentary Commissioner for Standards commenced his investigation of the matter in October 1996, at the request of the Committee on Standards and Privileges.

The Guardian defended the action, principally by entering full pleas of justification, in which the series of parliamentary questions and other interventions by Mr Hamilton and Mr Smith, and the series of payments allegedly made by Mr Al Fayed to Mr Hamilton and Mr Smith, and Mr Greer's alleged role as a conduit for some of those payments, were fully set out. May J stayed the action on the 21 July 1995 on the ground that the essential issues in the action could not be fairly or properly tried without infringing article 9 of the Bill of Rights 1689. There was no appeal. The action was revived in September 1996 after the coming into force (on the 4 September 1996) of section 13 of the Defamation Act 1996, and after Mr Hamilton had waived parliamentary privilege so far as concerned his conduct. In the result the action was never tried, because, very close to trial, it was dropped in circumstances which are not relevant for present purposes.

Reports of Parliamentary proceedings

At common law, no protection was given to those reporting speeches made in Parliament. The MP was absolutely privileged but the reporter and the publisher could face civil or criminal action. This was reflected in Stockdale v Hansard (1839) where libel damages were awarded against Hansard who had printed verbatim an authorised House of Commons report.

Protection is now afforded by the Parliamentary Papers Act 1840. Section 1 of this Act gives absolute protection against any civil or criminal action to anyone publishing papers by order of Parliament. If any proceedings based on such papers are initiated, these must be stayed on production of a certificate issued by the Speaker or Lord Chancellor.

Section 2 of the Act gives absolute protection to any copy of such paper. Section 3 only protects against actions of defamation in that it gives qualified privilege to extracts from any reports protected by ss.1 and 2. This means that such extracts are protected provided the defendant can show that they were published in good faith and without malice. This is reflected in the case of Dingle v Associated Newspapers (1960).

In this case, the plaintiff complained of an article written in the Daily Mail which included the reporting of a report of a Parliamentary select committee. The reporting of the select committee's report was privileged under the Parliamentary Papers Act 1840. At trial the judge held that the part of the article which reported on the proceedings in Parliament was privileged. The remainder of the article was found to be defamatory and the judge then set about fixing the damages for the libel. The court had to decide on how the responsibility might be apportioned.

Reports of Parliamentary proceedings are also protected by the ordinary law of defamation in so far as they are fair and accurate unless the defamed person can prove malice (Defamation Act 1996). The basis of this protection is that publication is deemed to be for the benefit of the public. In Cook v Alexander (1973) Lord Denning stated

" One may comment upon reports which are themselves the subject of privilege. A report to be fair and accurate must constitute a fair presentation of that which took place on the relevant occasion. It need not be a verbatim report. It can be selective and concentrate on one particular aspect as long as it reports fairly and accurately the impression that the reporter would have received as a reasonable spectator in the proceedings".

He further stated "He need not report it verbatim word for word or letter for letter and it is sufficient if it is a fair presentation of what took place so as to convey to the reader the impression which the debate itself would have made on a hearer of it. Test it this way: if a member of the house were asked: "What happened in the debate ? Tell me about it." His answer would be a sketch giving in words the impression it left on him, with more emphasis on one thing and less emphasis on another, just as it stuck in his memory."

Freedom from arrest
MP's have no privilege protecting them from arrest on criminal charges but are protected against arrest in connection with a civil matter while Parliament is in session and for 40 days before and after.

Parliament's right to determine its own composition
The Commons has the right to fill vacancies through by-elections. It can also determine the result, through an Election Committee, of

disputed elections. Parliament also has the right to determine whether members are legally disqualified. In the Case of Wedgewood Benn in 1961, the House of Commons refused to allow Tony Benn to take his seat although he had been duly elected. This is because he had succeeded to a peerage on the death of his father and was disqualified from sitting in the commons. In addition, Parliament may expel members whom it considers unfit to serve.

Right to regulate its own proceedings

Parliament is empowered to regulate its own internal proceedings. It may make standing orders to govern its procedures. The courts have always refused to consider whether these procedures have been complied with. In the case Pickin v British Rail Board (1974), it was alleged that the respondent had misled Parliament to secure the passing of a private Bill. The claimant said that the land taken from him under the Act was no longer required, and that he should be entitled to have it returned.

Held: When an enactment is passed there is finality unless and until it is amended or repealed by Parliament. Lord Morris of Borth-y-Gest said: "It must surely be for Parliament to lay down the procedures which are to be followed before a bill can become an Act. It must be for Parliament to decide whether its decreed procedures have in fact been followed. It must be for Parliament to lay down and to construe its standing orders and further to decide whether they have been obeyed; it must be for Parliament to decide whether in any particular case to dispense with compliance with such orders. It must be for Parliament to decide whether it is satisfied that an Act should be passed in the form and with the wording set out in the Act. It must be for Parliament to decide what documentary material or testimony it requires and the extent to which Parliamentary privilege should attach. It would be impracticable and undesirable for the High Court of Justice to embark on an enquiry concerning the effect or the effectiveness of the internal procedures in the High Court of Parliament or an enquiry whether in any particular case those procedures were effectively followed. Clear pronouncements on the law are to be found in a stream of authorities in the 19th century" and "it is the function of the courts to administer the laws which Parliament has enacted. In the processes of Parliament there will be much consideration whether a Bill should or should not in one form or another become an enactment. When an enactment is passed there is finality unless and until it is amended or repealed by Parliament. In the courts there may be argument as to the correct interpretation of the enactment: there must be none as to whether it should be on the statute book at all."

Punishment for contempt

The below have been held to be contempt of Parliament:

1. An attempt to interfere with the members freedom of action. In the NUPE case (1976/77) the national conference of NUPE passed a resolution demanding that the union's executive withdraw union sponsorship from those MP's who supported their parties public expenditure cuts. The Committee of Privileges found this to be a contempt but no action was taken when the General Secretary of the Union gave assurances that sanctions would not be imposed on MP's. Other attempts to obstruct MP's in the line of duty such as bribery or threats have constituted contempt.
2. Misconduct in the House or disobedience of the rules of the house.
3. Conduct of MP's in the House. For example, when John Profumo was found to have lied to the House (Profumo's case 1962/63) this was contempt. It follows that corruption, taking

bribes, failure to declare conflict of interests have all constituted contempts.

4. Publication of materials reflecting on the proceedings of the House and its members. This includes newspaper articles and criticising MP's. Publication of false reports of Parliamentary proceedings and ,premature disclosure of committee proceedings also constitute contempt.

Members can be suspended or expelled for contempt. Journalists can be suspended or expelled from the House for a period of time.

The financial interest of members

A number of incidents that took place in the 1990's, culminating in the "cash for questions" affair led to the establishment of the Nolan Committee into Standards in Public Life. This, in turn, led to the establishment of the Parliamentary Commissioner for Standards, a much more comprehensive register of member's interests, a reformed Committee of Standards and Privileges and a standing committee to enquire into standards in public life. The courts have refused to review the commissioners activities as they are concerned with matters within Parliament.

****

Ch. 7

Electoral law

The right to vote in an election

In the United Kingdom, at common law, anyone qualified to vote in an election has the right to do so and may bring a claim for damages in tort against any person who illegally excludes him. This was a principle arising out of the leading case of Ashby v White (1703). If a statute gives a right the common law will provide a remedy to maintain it where there is injury or damage. The courts jurisdiction to provide remedies for breaches of legal rights is not limited by parliamentary privilege.

Free elections

The principle of free elections was enacted by Article 8 Bill of Rights 1689, which provides that parliamentary elections ought to be free. Moreover, Article 3 European Convention on Human Rights and Fundamental Freedoms (1953) First Protocol, provides that the High Contracting Parties undertake to hold free elections at reasonable intervals by secret ballot, under conditions which will ensure the free expression of the opinion of the people in the choice of the legislature. This was incorporated into UK law by the Human Rights Act 1998.

The Franchise and the electorate

Essentially, the franchise is the legal right to vote and the electorate is all of those who have this right. The rules are to be found in the Representation of the People Act 1983, as amended by the Representation of the People Act 2000. To qualify to vote, an elector must be 18 years of age or over at the time of the election, be a British subject or citizen of the Republic of Ireland and not be subject to any legal disqualification. Any EU national may vote in elections for the European Parliament.

The Representation of the People Act 1989 allows UK citizens who live abroad to vote if they have been resident in the UK and registered as voters in the previous 20 years. Service personnel are entitled to be considered 'resident' providing that their absence results from service for the armed forces or the Crown overseas. Similar provisions apply for merchant seamen. The Representation of the People Act 2000 creates the concept of 'rolling' electoral registration. An electoral register for any given constituency will be produced for a specific election based on an annual return as amended by any subsequent changes. Section 3 of the 2000 Act deals with the residence requirements considered by registration officers when deciding whether or not to register a person as a voter. A person whose name is not on the register will not be entitled to vote. It is a criminal offence to vote in more than one constituency (other than as a proxy for another voter). Even if a person's name is on the register it is a criminal offence to vote if ineligible to do so. Those disqualified to vote include aliens, minors, mental defectives and drunkards. Under the 2000 Act, a person detained in a mental hospital as a voluntary patient may be registered as a voter provided his stay is sufficient for him to be regarded as a resident. Most convicted criminals are not eligible to vote. There is currently pressure by the EU on the UK to change this rule.

Constituencies
The changing or altering of constituencies is a matter for Parliament. Prior to the enactment of the Political parties, Elections and Referendums Act 2000, the determinations of constituency boundaries was undertaken by four Boundary Commissions for

England, Wales, Scotland and Northern Ireland. Under the 2000 Act that task is transferred to the Electoral Commission.

The Constituencies Act 2012

Sections 10 to 14 update and set out the current powers of the Boundary Commission. Section 11 of the Act provides that there shall be 600 constituencies within the United Kingdom of not more than 13,000 square kilometres unless it is at least 12,000 square kilometres and the Boundary Commission concerned is satisfied that it is not reasonably possible for the constituency to comply with that rule. The Act goes on to make further provisions for determining constituency boundaries.

Conduct of electoral campaigns: voting systems

The responsibility for the conduct of elections lies with the returning officer who is the Sheriff of the County or the Mayor of the Borough, depending on the constituency. Their authority is delegated to the registration officer for each constituency. Voting is by way of secret ballot. The candidate who receives the highest number of votes in each constituency is 'returned' as the MP for that constituency. There is no requirement that a candidate must obtain a minimum percentage of the total vote to be elected. This system of voting is known as the 'first past the post' system.

The vote to elect the mayor of London

This is known as the supplementary vote and is used to vote in the elections for Mayor of London. With the supplementary vote there are two columns on the ballot paper-one for the first choice and one for the second choice. Voters are not required to make a second choice if they do not wish to do so. First preferences are counted and if one candidate gets 50% of the vote then he or she is elected. If no candidate gets 50%, the two highest scoring candidates are retained and the rest of the candidates are eliminated. The second preferences on the ballot paper of the eliminated candidate are examined and any that have been cast for the two remaining candidates are given to them. Whoever has the most votes at the end of the process wins.

****

Ch. 8

The European Community and Public law

The main principle, or objective, of the European Community is the establishment of a common market. All Member States of the EC will be directly affected by the common market, as will individuals in those states. See end of chapter for details of The Referendum of 2016 and the decision to exit the EU.

One of the earliest cases that reinforces this is Van Gend en Loos v Nederlandse Administratie Der Belastinge (case 26/62) 1963. In this case, Van Gend en Loos, a firm of importers were required to pay customs duty on a product imported from Germany, under a law adopted after the creation of the (then) EEC. The importers challenged the payment on the basis that the extra duty infringed Article 25 of the Treaty (see below) which prohibited the introduction of new customs duties. The Dutch Court referred the question to the European Court of Justice under Article 234. It was held that the EC is a new legal order in international law, on behalf of which states have limited their sovereign rights and whose subjects comprise not only states but individuals. Article 25 of the treaty produces direct effects in the relationship between the Member States and their subjects, creating individual rights which the national courts must protect.

The background to the European Community from 1957

The present European Community (EC) and the European Union (EU) have their origins in the European Economic Community

(EEC) created by the Treaty of Rome in 1957. This original treaty provided the basis for a customs union and what is known as the common market, which is the free movement of goods, people, services and money for the original six signatory states. Those states were Germany, France, Italy, Belgium, the Netherlands and Luxembourg. In addition, as we have also seen, the same states also formed the European Coal and Steel Community (ECSC) and the European Atomic Energy Authority (Euratom).

Later, in 1973, the United Kingdom, Denmark and Ireland took up membership. The UK's membership was against the well-documented backdrop of dissent. The United Kingdom has enacted the European Communities Act in 1972 to give effect to its obligations under EC law. Later on, other countries joined, Greece 1981, Spain 1986, Portugal 1986 and Austria, Sweden and Finland in 1995. Many other countries have gained membership since 1995.

The main institutions of the EU

There exist five main institutions which carry out the main tasks of the European Community:

- The Council of Ministers-an ad hoc body of ministers from the Member states responsible for the adoption of legislation
- The Commission-a permanent body which proposes legislation and also has a monitoring role in relation to the implementation of EC law
- The European Parliament
- The Court of Justice-this court is the final authority on matters of European Community law, assisted by the Court of First Instance
- The Court of Auditors

The Treaties

The main point about the European Community Treaty, in its various stages, is that it is an integral part of the legal system of the Member States and, as such, must be applied in their courts.

One of the earliest cases challenging the legitimacy of the EC Treaty is that of Costa v ENEL (Case 6/64) 1964. In this case the nationalised Italian Electricity Company (ENEL) had been created in 1962. Costa refused to pay his bill on the grounds that the nationalisation infringed the Italian Constitution and also various provisions of the treaty. It was held by the European Court of Justice, in this case, that the transfer by Member States from their domestic legal systems to the EC system of rights and responsibilities carries with it a permanent limitation of their sovereign rights, against which a later unilateral act incompatible with EC law cannot prevail.

The original European Economic Community Treaty was amended in 1986 by the Single European Act (SEA). It was also further amended in 1993 by the Treaty on European Union (Maastricht Treaty) and the 1997 Treaty of Amsterdam (ToA). The Single European Act created the mechanism to complete the single, or internal, market. This is an area without internal frontiers within which goods, services, people and money can circulate freely.

The Treaty on European Union created a structure based on three pillars:

1) the EC
2) the Common Foreign and Security Policy
3) Police and Judicial Co-operation

The first pillar, the EC, is governed by law under the EC Treaty, the second and third pillars are administered through intergovernmental co-operation. The Maastricht Treaty provided for both political and monetary union (EMU). The single currency came into effect on January 1st 1999.

The United Kingdom, through protocols annexed to the treaty, opted out of EMU and, at the time of the Maastricht Treaty, of the Agreement on Social Policy (known as the Social Chapter) which established a legal base for certain types of employment protection.

Ratification of all member states of the Maastricht Treaty was completed in 1999, May 1st, this being the date that the Treaty Amendments came into force. The Treaty of Amsterdam introduced into the treaty an Employment Chapter, requiring member states to co-ordinate their economic policies, focussing on growth and employment.

The European Court of Justice now has jurisdiction in certain areas relating to police and judicial co-operation (the third pillar). The Social Chapter was incorporated into the body of the revised Treaty following the change of government in the UK in 1997. Article 13 of the Treaty provides the basis for action to combat discrimination on the grounds of gender, race, religion, sexual orientation or disability. Sanctions can be imposed on member states for infringements of human rights.

The Schengen Agreement
The revised treaty also incorporated the **Schengen Agreement.** Member states agreed to relax border formalities on the movement of people. The United Kingdom and Ireland have opted out of this part of the treaty. Following the signing of the Treaty of Nice in February 2001, the Treaty came into force on February 2003.

The Treaty of Nice

The Treaty of Nice paved the way for a significant enlargement of the European Community, taking in a large number of mainly Eastern European states. As a result of the newly enlarged EU, with a virtual doubling of its Members, the current EU is a different body to the previous one. Major changes are required and are now in process. The Treaty of Nice sets out principles and methods to change the system as the EU expands. For example, changes to the composition of the Commission and weighted voting in the council applied from 2005 and changes in the number of MEP's applied from the elections in 2004.

In December 2001, the Laeken European Council issued a Declaration leading to the setting up of the European Convention, which involved existing Member States and applicant states in discussion about the EU. The Convention on the Future of Europe took place in March 2002 and closed in March 2003. The resultant treaty arising from these sessions was rejected, due to continuing differences over qualified voting in the Council.

Ten new Member States joined the EU on May 1st 2004-the Czech Republic, Estonia, Latvia, Cyprus, Lithuania, Hungary, Malta, Poland, Slovenia and Slovakia. In the absence of a new treaty, institutional changes were governed by the provisions of the various acts of accession and the Treaty of Nice. In 2007, further Member States have been added, Romania and Bulgaria with plans to add more, notably Albania. The UK has adopted a different set of criteria in relation to these countries with regard to the right to work and settle in the UK.

In October of 2004, in Rome, agreement was eventually reached, and signed, on a Constitutional Treaty for the EU. However, the

Member States were unable to reach agreement on this and in its place came the Lisbon Treaty.

The Lisbon Treaty

The Lisbon Treaty was signed by the heads of state and government of the 27 EU Member States on 13th December 2007. It is intended to reform the functioning of the European Union following the two waves of enlargement that have taken place since 2004 and which have increased the number of EU Member States from 15 to 27.

The Lisbon treaty was drafted as a replacement for the Constitutional treaty which was rejected by French and Dutch voters in 2005.

The Lisbon Treaty includes key changes aimed at increasing the consistency and coherence of the EU's external actions. It provides for a so called 'High Representative of the Union for Foreign Affairs and Security Policy'. The High Representative will chair the EU's External Relations Council and he or she will also be a vice president of the European Commission. The High representative will be responsible for coordinating the Commissions external actions in order to ensure consistency between all of EU external actions, whether they are under the competence of the Council or Commission.

The High Representative will be supported by a European External Action Service. The detailed role, function and composition of this service is still under discussion. It will be made up of officials from both the Council and the Commission as well as civil servants from the EU Member States. In addition to the above mentioned institutional changes, the Lisbon Treaty also provides for a number of changes to the EU's external policies. It both strengthens and clarifies the EU's development cooperation policy and, for the first time, sets out humanitarian assistance as a specific Commission competence. One significant change set out in the Lisbon Treaty is: Reforming the system of Council presidencies from its current six month rotation to appointing a full time Council President for a period of two and a half years.

The Treaty of Lisbon made the European Council a formal institution distinct from the Council of the EU, and created the present permanent presidency. The Council of the EU retains the rotation of president, with no change to powers, but the new system entails the appointment of the president for two and a half years instead of six months, as previously.

In December 2009, the European Council elected its first president, Herman Van Rumpoy.

Other changes include:

- Reducing the number of Commissioners (applicable from 2014);
- Changing the weighting of votes by Member States (from 2014; and
- Extending the scope of qualified majority voting to new areas.

The Lisbon Treaty is now ratified by all 27 Member States and entered into force on 1st December 2009.

Structure of the Lisbon Treaty
The Lisbon Treaty is divided into two parts: The Treaty on European Union and the Treaty on the Functioning of the European Union.

The Treaty on European Union sets out the general provisions governing the European Union. It also sets out the overall provisions of the EU's external relations.

The Treaty on the Functioning of the European Union covers cooperation with third countries and humanitarian aid.

As mentioned at the beginning of the chapter, the United Kingdom has, via a referendum, decided to leave the EU (BREXIT).

What is Brexit?

The people of Britain voted for a British exit, or Brexit, from the EU in a historic referendum on Thursday June 23 2016. Prime Minister Theresa May triggered Article 50 - the step that starts the timer on two years of Brexit talks - on Wednesday March 29 2017. Mrs May was given the power to trigger Article 50 when the Queen signed off on the Brexit bill .

Britain is planning to leave the EU's single market to regain control over immigration and end the supremacy of EU laws. The Prime Minister advocates a clean break from the EU and rejects any watered-down departure deal that leaves the UK "half in and half out" of the EU.

MPs overwhelming voted to pass the Brexit bill and rejected changes made by Europhile peers in the House of Lords. It came after the Supreme Court upheld a High Court ruling that there must be a Parliamentary vote before triggering Article 50.

MPs and peers will be given another vote on the final EU deal after two years of Brexit talks come to an end. On the day of Brexit, the Great Repeal Bill will come into force and end the supremacy of EU law over Britain's own legislation.

Brexiteers have argued that Britain is now free to take back control of its borders in order to curb immigration and increase security. The UK will no longer have to accept 'free movement of people' from Europe because it is preparing to leave the EU's single market.

****

Ch.9

Human Rights in UK law

Before the Human Rights Act (HRA) 1998, civil and political rights were recognised and enforced in the United Kingdom solely within the established framework of statutory and common law principles. During the twentieth century human rights principles were developed in international law by treaties and international organisations.

The Council of Europe drafted the European Convention on Human Rights and Fundamental Freedoms to guarantee basic civil and political rights, which have been expanded by a series of supplementary treaties called protocols, and provide a judicial system for their enforcement.

The Human Rights Act 1998 incorporates Convention rights into UK law. It creates new rules of statutory interpretation, enables citizens to test the compatibility of legislation with Convention rights, and obliges the courts to take 'Strasbourg principles' into account when considering human rights issues in litigation.

The European Convention on Human Rights and Fundamental Freedoms

The European Convention on Human Rights and Fundamental Freedoms guarantees civil and political rights. These rights consist of:

- the right to life
- prohibition of torture

- inhuman or degrading treatment or punishment
- prohibition of slavery and forced labour
- right to liberty
- right to a fair and unbiased hearing
- the prohibition of retrospective legislation
- the right to private and family life
- freedom of conscience and religion
- freedom of expression
- freedom of association
- the right to marry and found a family

The Convention on Human Rights has been supplemented and amended by a series of additional treaties called protocols. The First and Sixth Protocols give individuals additional rights which were incorporated into British law by the HRA 1998. The First Protocol covers protection of property, the right to education and the right to free elections. The Sixth and Twelfth Protocols cover the abolition of the death penalty.

Using the Convention against public authorities

It is unlawful for a public authority to act in a way which is incompatible with a Convention right. This provision is contained in s 6(1) of the 1998 Act. A public authority, according to section 6(3) includes a court or tribunal and also any person certain of whose functions are the functions of a public authority. It does not, according to section 6(3) include either Houses of Parliament or a person exercising functions in connection with proceedings in Parliament.

The meaning of 'public authority' was discussed in the case of L v Birmingham City Council (2008) when the question was whether the owners and proprietors of a care home who took people on behalf of a local authority was a public authority for the purpose of s6 HRA 1998. The finding was that the provision of care and accommodation by a private company, as opposed to its regulation and supervision under statutory rules, is not an inherently public function and fell outside the ambit of s(3)(b) of the HRA 1998.

Under s 7(1) any victim, or would be victim, of an unlawful act under s 6(1) may bring proceedings against the authority in any appropriate court or tribunal, or rely on the convention rights concerned in any legal proceedings.

Proceedings must, under s 7(5) be brought within one year beginning with the date on which the act complained of took place; or such longer period which the court or tribunal thinks equitable under all the circumstances.

The extent of a person's right to rely on a breach of a Convention right was discussed by the House of Lords in Matthews v Ministry of Defence (2003). In this case, the claimant claimed damages in the tort of negligence. The defendant sought to escape liability by relying on s 10 Crown Proceedings Act 1947. The case raised a preliminary issue as to whether s 10 of the act was compatible with the right to a fair trial contained in Article 6 European Convention of Human Rights and Fundamental Freedoms. The principle from this case was that although the meaning of 'civil rights' in Article 6 of the Convention is an autonomous concept and cannot be interpreted solely by reference to domestic law, a litigants right of access to the court under Article 6 (1) applies only to civil rights which could, on arguable grounds, be recognised under domestic law and where the restriction on the right of access was procedural in nature.

It was held that s10 imposed a limitation which operated not as a procedural bar but as a matter of substantive law under which the claimant had no civil right to which Article 6 might apply.

Remedies

If a public authority has breached a Convention right, the remedy, which the court can grant to the victim is covered by s8. The remedies available under s8(1) are damages, declarations, injunctions, quashing orders, mandatory orders and prohibiting orders.

Damages

The availability of damages under s 8 was discussed by the House of Lords in Marcic v Thames Water Utility (2004) in which the defendant was a statutory sewage undertaker under the Water Industry Act 1991 and as such a public authority under s 6(3) HRA 1998 and the claimant a householder whose premises were regularly flooded with sewage. He claimed damages in nuisance and under the HRA 1998. The principle from this case was that where a public authority is subject to an elaborate statutory scheme of regulation, which includes an independent regulator with powers of enforcement whose decisions are subject to judicial review, there is no claim for damages under s 6(1) HRA 1998. It was held that the claimant had no claim for damages against Thames Water.

Another key case which determined the approach to awarding damages in human rights cases was Anufrijeva v Southwark (2004). The Court of Appeal had to consider the rules determining awards of damages in England and Wales where s8 Convention rights are engaged. The principle from this case was that the approach to awarding damages in this jurisdiction should be no less liberal than those applied by the European Court of Human Rights or one of the purposes of the HRA will be defeated and claimants will be still be put to the expense of having to go to Strasbourg to obtain justice.

Under s8 HRA 1998, damages can be awarded on the basis of what is necessary and appropriate to give just satisfaction. Damages should be modest and proportionate.

The focus of the European Convention on Human Rights and Fundamental Freedoms is the protection of human rights rather than awards of compensation. The European Court, for example, will award damages only where it is satisfied that the loss or damage complained of is actually caused by the violation. Awards of compensation for anxiety and frustration attributable to the article 6 violation suffered are made very sparingly and for modest sums.

Declarations of incompatibility

Section 4 of the HRA 1998 creates the 'declaration of incompatibility'. The most important effect of making a declaration is that it puts pressure on the government to change the law. The courts which have the power to make such declarations are the House of Lords (Supreme Court), the Judicial Committee of the Privy Council, the Courts Martial Appeal Court, the High Court of Justiciary, the Court of Sessions, the High Court and the Court of Appeal. Principles of incompatibility were discussed by the Court of Appeal in Wilson v First County Trust Ltd (No 2) (2001). The Court of Appeal ordered a hearing in order to determine whether to make a declaration of incompatibility under s 4(2) HRA 1998 that s127 Consumer Credit Act 1974 was incompatible with Article 6 ECHR and Article 1 of the First Protocol in that it barred a creditor from enforcing a loan agreement. Since October 1st 2000, the court is required by the provisions of the HRA 1998 to avoid acting in a way which is incompatible with a Convention right. The court must consider:

o The facts as they were at the time when it made the order and whether that obligation is affected by s22(4) HRA 1998, which prevents a claimant from relying on the 1998 Act where a public authority has acted incompatibly with a Convention right prior to 1st October 1998

o The relevant date for deciding whether s22(4) applies is the date the court made the order.

The court had power to make a declaration of incompatibility pursuant to s4 HRA 1998.

The principles governing declarations of incompatibility were developed further in R (Alconbury Developments Limited) v Secretary of State for the Environment, Transport and the Regions (2001). The House of Lords laid down the following principles: to determine whether civil rights under Article 6(1) ECHR are involved in a claim, the court must look at the relevant jurisprudence of the European Court of Human Rights; decisions taken by a Secretary of State are compatible with Article 6(1) provided they are reviewable by an independent and impartial tribunal which has full jurisdiction to deal with the case as the nature of the decision requires.

Brexit - will decisions of the European Court of Justice and the European Court of Human Rights Be Affected?

Whilst much has been made by the 'leave' campaigners about the fact that Brexit will impact on interference by the European Court of Human Rights (ECtHR) in decisions of the UK courts, this is not correct.

Whether we exit the EU or not, this will not affect the fact that the UK is bound by common law which implies many fundamental rights,and we also signed up the the European Convention on

Human Rights ('ECHR') before the EU even existed. We are one of 47 nations (including Russia) to have signed up to the Council of Europe which is entirely independent of the EU and which administers the ECHR. We also have primary legislation in the UK called the Human Rights Act 1998 which specifically incorporates the ECHR

To be free of the interference of the ECHR we would have to repeal/amend the Human Rights Act and remove ourselves from the Council of Europe and the ECHR . Two recent employment cases have shown us that whilst similar arguments can be brought in two separate European Courts, one of them would automatically be affected in the event that Britain votes to leave the EU on 23 June 2016 and the other will not. Both involved dress codes and both involved the right to visibly display signs of faith, but argued in different ways:

Eweida v United Kingdom

Article 9 of the European Convention for the Protection of Human Rights and Fundamental Freedoms says that employees have the right to visibly display signs of their faith and Article 14 which says they should be free from discrimination in the exercise of this freedom.

Ms Eweida was, in breach of those rights, prevented from wearing a cross at work, as a Christian, because BA had (but has since changed) a corporate dress code banning the wearing of jewellry on the grounds of maintaining their corporate image.

The ECtHR agreed with Ms Eweida, saying that the ban was not proportionate and the UK courts had given too much weight to the need for BA to maintain its corporate image, especially given the lack of any evidence to support the fact that a discrete cross had any effect on the corporate image or encroached on the interests of others.

If the UK left the EU, Ms Eweida would still have been able to bring her claim before the ECtHR under the ECHR.

Achbita v G4S

In 1973 the UK gave up the right to have the final say in relation to employment and discrimination law. UK courts must have regard to European treaties, laws and decisions of the European Court of Justice ('ECJ') when bringing in legislation and making decisions. All discrimination law (except for equal pay) is contained within three EU Directives and the UK Government is expected to bring in and enforce laws which reflect these.

Whilst this was a case in Belgium, it could just as easily have been one in the UK: Ms Achbita was a Muslim receptionist in Belgium who wanted to wear an Islamic headscarf but G4S had rules banning employees wearing any religious, political or philosophical symbols while on duty, to ensure neutrality at work. The Belgium Court of Appeal asked the ECJ to rule on whether a ban on female Muslim employees wearing a headscarf at work constituted direct discrimination contrary to EU law? It was accepted that although indirect discriminatory, it could probably be justified given the policy of neutrality.

The ECJ's Advocate General has given her opinion, which the ECJ can either agree with or ignore. She said that it was not direct discrimination and even if it had been, the ban could be justified under the 'genuine and determining occupational requirement' exemption. She believed that it was proportionate to require compliance with a dress code that gave effect to the employer's strict policy of neutrality but it would be for the courts in Belgium to

91

consider whether the policy in fact caused undue prejudice to employees taking various factors into consideration.

If this had been a UK case, then Britain leaving the EU would fundamentally affect the outcome of this case because if we left, the final view of the ECJ would be irrelevant as the UK would no longer have surrendered sovereignty to the EU on these points. The practical effect would be that the Supreme Court in the UK will have the final word in cases.

Therefore, as leaving the EU is unlikely to have any effect on challenges through the ECtHR, perhaps more cases will be heading in that direction as a result?

****

Ch.10

Police Organisation

Rather than having one national police force, the UK has 43 police forces. These are independent locally run police forces, designed to forge links between the police and local communities. Working alongside police officers are Community Support officers (CSO's) civilians employed by police authorities. Their powers include the ability to:

- issue fixed penalty notices for anti-social behaviour
- carry out searches and road checks
- stop and detain school truants
- deprive an individual of their liberty for up to 30 minutes until a police officer arrives, where the suspect fails to provide his name and address or it is reasonably suspected that the details provided are inaccurate.

The Serious Crime and Police Act 2005 created a national investigation agency, The Serious Organised Crime Agency (SOCA) to tackle the heads of organised crime who undertake illegal enterprises such as drug trafficking, paedophile rings and people smuggling. As of October 2013, following the introduction of the Crime and Courts Act 2013,, SOCA has been replaced by the National Crime Agency

Over time, there has been a general increase in recorded crime, with violent crime on the increase. The police are obviously in the front line dealing with crime as a whole. The main police powers are contained within the Police and Criminal Evidence Act (PACE)

1984 with amendments and additions made by the Criminal Justice and Public Order Act 1994 and the Criminal Justice Act 2003. PACE also provides for the codes of practice giving extra details on the procedures for stop and search, detaining, questioning and identifying suspects. These are issued by the Home Secretary.

Police powers

The police have to exercise their powers sensitively and respect the rights of the individual citizen. At the same time they must also have sufficient powers to enable them to do their job. The law on police powers is mainly contained within the Police and Criminal Evidence Act 1984 and the associated codes of practice contained within section 66 of the Act. There are six codes:

- Code A deals with the powers to stop and search
- Code B for the powers to search premises and seize property
- Code C deals with detention, treatment and questioning of subjects
- Code D deals with the rules for identification procedures
- Code E deals with the tape recording of interviews with suspects
- Code F deals with visual recording of interviews
- Code G applies to any arrest made by a police officer from January 2006
- Code H revised code of practice in connection with detention, treatment and questioning by police officers under the Terrorism Act 2000.

These codes are constantly revised and should be double checked.

Powers to arrest-serious arrestable offences

Some of the rules only apply to serious arrestable offences. These include murder, treason, manslaughter, rape, hijacking, kidnapping, hostage taking, drug trafficking, firearms offences and causing explosions likely to endanger life or property. Other arrestable offences may only be considered to be serious if they endanger the state or public order or cause death of a person.

Powers to stop and search

The powers of police to stop and search people or vehicles are contained in sections 1-7 of PACE. Section 1 gives police the powers to stop and search people and vehicles in a public place. A public place has a wide meaning and extends to private gardens if the police officer in question has good reason to believe that the suspect does not live at that address. To use this power under PACE the police officer must have reasonable grounds for suspecting that the person is in possession of stolen goods or prohibited articles or goods. These include knives and other weapons which can cause harm or be used in burglary or theft.

Voluntary searches

This is where a person is prepared to submit to a search voluntarily. A voluntary search can only take place where there is power to search anyway. Voluntary searches must be recorded.

Other powers to stop and search

Apart from PACE there are also other Acts of Parliament which give the police the right to stop and search in special circumstances. The Misuse of Drugs Act 1971 allows the police to search for controlled drugs and the Anti-Terrorism, Crime and Security Act 2001 gives powers to stop and search where there is reasonable suspicion of involvement in terrorism. Section 60 of the Criminal Justice and Public Order Act 1994 gives the police an additional power of the right to stop and search in anticipation of violence.

Roadside checks

Section 4 of PACE gives police the right to stop and search vehicles if there is a reasonable suspicion that a person who has committed a serious offence is at large in an area.

The power to search premises

In certain circumstances the police have the power to enter and search premises. PACE sets out most of these powers although there are other Acts which provide for this.

The police can enter a premises without the occupiers permission if a warrant authorising that search has been obtained from a magistrate. This will normally be issued under section 8 of PACE. The magistrate must be convinced that the police have reasonable grounds for believing that a serious arrestable offence has been committed and that there is material on the premises that will be of substantial value in the investigation of the offence. Search warrants are designed to enable the element of surprise and in the process prevent valuable evidence being removed or destroyed.

A warrant must specify the premises to be searched and, as far as possible, the articles or persons to be sought. One entry only, on one occasion is authorised and entry must be at a reasonable hour unless the police can demonstrate the need to enter at another time. They are also required to identify themselves as police officers and to show the warrant on demand. The courts have, however, held that the police do not have to follow these requirements precisely if the circumstances of the case make it appropriate to do otherwise.

Powers to enter premises without a search warrant

Police officers may enter and search premises if it is in order to arrest a person named in an arrest warrant, or to arrest someone for an arrestable offence, or to recapture an escaped prisoner. This power is set out in section 17 of PACE. Reason for the entry must be given to anyone in the premises. PACE also gives a police officer the right to enter a premises without a search warrant after an arrest if an officer has grounds to believe that there is evidence on the premises relating to the offence for which the person has just been arrested.

To prevent a breach of the peace

There is a right under common law for police to enter premises if there is a need to deal with or prevent a breach of the peace. This right applies even to private homes as was demonstrated by the case of McLeod v Commissioner of Police for the Metropolis (1994) in which the police had entered domestic premises when there was a violent quarrel taking place. See next chapter on Public Order for more information on police powers to prevent a breach of the peace.

Searching with the consent of the occupier of the premises

The police may enter and search a premises without a warrant if the occupier of these premises gives them permission to do so. This consent must be given in writing and can be withdrawn.

Unlawful entry and search

If a premises is entered and searched unlawfully, where the police exceed their powers a claim for damages can be made under the tort of trespass.

Powers of arrest

Section 24 of PACE sets out the general powers of arrest, and some of these powers can be exercised by private citizens as well as the police.

Arrestable offences

An arrestable offence is:

1. Any offence for which the sentence is fixed by law. An example may be murder which has a fixed term of life imprisonment.
2. Any offence for which the maximum sentence that could be given to an adult is five years imprisonment.
3. Any other offence which Parliament has specifically made an arrestable offence.

PACE Section 24-Arrests by police and private citizens

This section allows the police or a private citizen to arrest without a warrant:

1. Anyone who is in the act of committing an arrestable offence
2. Anyone whom he has reasonable grounds for suspecting to be committing an arrestable offence
3. Anyone who has committed an arrestable offence
4. Where an arrestable offence has been committed, anyone for whom he has reasonable grounds for suspecting to be guilty of it.

The police also have the right to arrest anyone who is about to commit an arrestable offence, anyone whom he has reasonable grounds for suspecting to be about to commit an arrestable offence or where there are reasonable grounds for suspecting that an arrestable offence has been committed.

PACE Section 25

Police have further powers under section 25 to arrest for any offence where the suspects name and address cannot be discovered or that there are reasonable grounds to believe that the name and address given by the suspect are false. Section 25 also provides powers of arrest where there are reasonable grounds for believing that arrest is necessary to prevent that person from:

- Causing physical injury to himself or others
- Suffering physical injury (i.e. suicide)
- Causing loss or damage to property
- Committing an offence against public decency
- Causing an unlawful obstruction of the highways

Section 25 also gives the police powers to arrest if the arrest is believed to be necessary to protect a child or other vulnerable person.

Other rights of arrest

The Criminal Justice and Public Order Act 1994 added an extra power of arrest to PACE. This is in section 46A of PACE and gives the police the right to arrest without a warrant anyone who has been released on police bail and fails to attend a police station at an allotted time. The Criminal Justice and Public Order Act also gives police the right to arrest for a variety of new offences in connection with collective or aggravated trespass.

Arrest for breach of the peace

The police have a right to arrest where there has been or is likely to be a breach of the peace. The conditions for arrest for breach of the peace were laid down in Bibby v Chief Constable of Essex Police (2000). These are:

- There must be sufficiently real and present threat to the peace
- The threat must come from the person to be arrested

- The conduct of the person must clearly interfere with the rights of others and its natural consequence must be 'not wholly unreasonable' violence from a third party
- The conduct of the person to be arrested must be unreasonable

The right to search an arrested person

Where a person has been arrested the police have a right to search that person for anything which might be used to help an escape or anything that might be evidence relating to an offence.

Powers to detain suspect

Once a person has been arrested and taken to a police station there are rules setting out time limits as to detention. The limits will vary and are longer depending on the severity of the offence. There are also rules, contained in PACE relating to treatment of people in detention.

The general rules are that the police may detain a person for 24 hours. After this the police can detain a person for a further 12 hours but only with the permission of a senior officer. After 36 hours those detained for an ordinary arrestable offence must be released or charged. For serious offences those detained can be held for a further period but a magistrates order must be obtained and the maximum detention cannot exceed 96 hours. There is a right to representation. There is an exception under terrorism offences which allows for detention of 48 hours and up to another 12 days with the Home Secretary's permission .(See next chapter).

Rights of detained people

Detainees must be informed of their rights. These include:

- Someone must/can be informed of the arrest

- Being told that independent legal advice is freely available and being allowed to consult with a solicitor
- Being allowed to consult the code of practice

Police interviews

Detained persons may be interviewed by the police. All interviews carried out at a police station must be tape recorded. Suspects have the right to a solicitor during questioning. If a solicitor is not asked for or is late questioning can commence. If the person is under 17 or is mentally handicapped there must be an 'appropriate adult' present during questioning. Section 76 of PACE states that a court shall not allow statements which have been obtained through oppression to be used as evidence.

The right to silence

A defendant has the right to remain silent but inferences can be drawn from the silence and used in court. The wording of a caution given to a suspect states:

'You do not have to say anything. But it may harm your defence if you do not mention when questioned something which you later rely on in court. Anything you do say may be given in evidence'

Searches, fingerprints and samples

When a person is being held at a police station the police do not have an automatic right to search them. However, a custody officer has a duty to record everything a person has with them and if the custody officer thinks a search is necessary then a non-intimate search can be made. A strip search can only take place if it is necessary to remove an article which a person in detention should not be allowed to keep and there is reasonable suspicion that a person may have concealed an article. There are strict rules governing the nature of a strip search and articles of clothing that can be removed at once and in which places.

The police can take fingerprints and non-intimate body samples without the persons consent. Reasonable force can be used to obtain these if necessary. There are different rules for intimate samples. These are defined in the Criminal Justice and Public Order Act 1994 as:

a) a sample of blood, semen or other tissue, fluid, urine or public hair
b) a dental impression
c) a swab taken from a person's body orifice other than the mouth

These can only be taken by a registered medical practitioner or nurse. Samples can be retained.

Complaints against the police
People who believe that the police have acted unjustly and exceeded their powers can complain and the type of complaint will determine how it is dealt with. Minor complaints are dealt with informally and more serious complaints will be dealt with at a higher level.

The Independent Police Complaints Commission
This was set up in 2004 to supervise the handling of complaints against the police and associated staff, such as Community Support Officers. The IPCC sets down standards for the police to follow when dealing with complaints. They also monitor the way complaints are dealt with by local police forces. The IPCC will also investigate serious issues including any accident involving death or serious injury, allegations of corruption, allegations against senior

officers, allegations involving racism and allegations of perverting the course of justice.

Any member of the public can complain and complaints can be made directly to the IPCC or through organisations such as the Citizens Advice Bureau or through the Commission for Equality and Human Rights or the Youth Offending Team. It is also possible to complain through a solicitor or an MP. Where the police have committed a crime in the execution of their duties criminal action can be brought against them.

****

Ch.11

Public Order

The right to demonstrate against unpopular causes is considered to be an inalienable right in the United Kingdom. However, given that the UK does not have a written constitution there has been no such positive statment from government and the lawmakers. The approach taken is that any interference with individual liberty must be justified in terms of law or statute. This is reflected in the case of Entick v Carrington (1756).

On 11 November 1762, the King's Chief Messenger, Nathan Carrington, and three other King's messengers, James Watson, Thomas Ardran, and Robert Blackmore, broke into the home of the Grub-street writer, John Entick in the parish of St Dunstan, Stepney "with force and arms". Over the course of four hours, they broke open locks and doors and searched all of the rooms before taking away 100 charts and 100 pamphlets, causing £2000 of damage. The King's messengers were acting on the orders of Lord Halifax, newly appointed Secretary of State for the Northern Department, "to make strict and diligent search for . . . the author, or one concerned in the writing of several weekly very seditious papers entitled, The Monitor, or British Freeholder".

Entick sued the messengers for trespassing on his land.

Judgment

The trial took place in Westminster Hall presided over by Lord Camden, the Chief Justice of the Common Pleas. Carrington and his colleagues claimed that they acted on Halifax's warrant, which gave them legal authority to search Entick's home; they therefore could not be liable for the tort. However, Camden held that Halifax had no right under statute or under precedent to issue such a warrant and therefore found in Entick's favour. In the most famous passage Camden stated:

" The great end, for which men entered into society, was to secure their property. That right is preserved sacred and incommunicable in all instances, where it has not been taken away or abridged by some public law for the good of the whole. The cases where this right of property is set aside by private law, are various. Distresses, executions, forfeitures, taxes etc are all of this description; wherein every man by common consent gives up that right, for the sake of justice and the general good. By the laws of England, every invasion of private property, be it ever so minute, is a trespass. No man can set his foot upon my ground without my license, but he is liable to an action, though the damage be nothing; which is proved by every declaration in trespass, where the defendant is called upon to answer for bruising the grass and even treading upon the soil. If he admits the fact, he is bound to show by way of justification, that some positive law has empowered or excused him. The justification is submitted to the judges, who are to look into the books; and if such a justification can be maintained by the text of the statute law, or by the principles of common law. If no excuse can be found or produced, the silence of the books is an authority against the defendant, and the plaintiff must have judgment. "

Hence Lord Camden ruled, as later became viewed as a general principle, that the state may do nothing but that which is expressly authorised by law, while the individual may do anything but that which is forbidden by law.

Significance

The judgment established the limits of executive power in English law: the state can only act lawfully in a manner prescribed by statute or common law. An assembly or procession was not unlawful *per se*, unless, for example, it caused an obstruction or constituted a public nuisance. Prior permission was not required for a demonstration unless it was being held on private land or in some special location regulated by specific byelaws such as Trafalgar Square.

Over the years, legislation has been introduced which imposes more specific boundaries and regulates the act of demonstrating. A raft of legislation was enacted during the Conservative administrations 1979-2007. The relevant statutes in place now are The Public Order Act 1986, the Criminal Justice and Public Order Act 1995, the Anti-social Behaviour Act 2003 and the Serious Organized Crime and Police Act 2005.

In addition to domestic legislation the passage of the European Convention on Human Rights has had a significant impact on law in the UK.

Article 11 of the ECHR

Article 11 of the ECHR says that everyone has the right of peaceful assembly and to freedom of association with others. No restriction shall be placed upon these rights other than those that are prescribed at law and are necessary in a democratic society in the interests of national security or public safety for the prevention of disorder or crime, for the protection of health or morals or the protection of the rights and freedom of others. In addition, Article 10 of the ECHR provides that everyone has the right to freedom of expression, subject to the same qualifications. Thus the right to demonstrate peacefully has now been recognised in positive terms. Any restrictions must be proportionate. This change of approach was anticipated in the significant case of DPP v Jones (HL 1999) following a peaceful protest on the highway near Stonehenge. This important case establishes that the right of the public to use the highway extends to the right to peaceful assembly, so long as the assembly does not obstruct the highway. The prosecution in the case had tried to argue that the defendants were in breach of an order made under Section 14A of the Public Order Act 1986 prohibiting 'trespassory assemblies' from taking place. It was ruled that in the particular circumstances of this case, use of the highway did not amount to trespass and that therefore the defendants were not in breach.

Location of meetings and demonstrations

Any meetings on private premises must have the consent of the owner. In a landmark case, The European Court of Human Rights held that there had been no violation of Article 10 in Appleby and others v. the United Kingdom (2003)

The town centre of Washington, known as the "Galleries", was originally built by a corporation set up by the government of the UK. It was then sold to Postel Properties Limited, a privately owned company. Development plans for the surrounding area included building over the only available playing field in the vicinity.

Mrs. Appleby, Mrs. Beresford, Mr. Alphonsus, and an environmental group, Washington First Forum, set up stands collecting signatures of protest at the entrance of the Galleries which they had to close because of security reasons. As they wanted to continue collecting signatures, they applied to Postel Properties Limited for permission to set up stands inside the shopping centre which they were denied.

Postel Properties Limited argued that the Town Centre is privately owned and they wished to stay neutral on all political and religious issues, relying on their right in Common Law to exclude or invite anyone unto their property without having to justify their conduct.

Mrs. Appleby and the other applicants then claimed that the exclusion from the shopping centre violated their right to freedom of expression (Article 10 European Convention on Human Rights), supporting their claim by citing Canadian and US cases as comparisons. They argued that the state was directly responsible as it was a public entity that had built the Galleries on public land and a minister who had approved the transfer into private ownership.

The judgement found no violation of Article 10 of the European Convention on Human Rights. As the shopping centre was privately owned, the authorities did not bear any direct responsibility for this restriction on the applicants' freedom of expression. Although shopping centres are gradually replacing the traditional town centres thus becoming "quasi-public spaces", the applicants were in the present case not restricted to obtain permission from the individual shop-owners or collecting the signatures elsewhere. Thus, their freedom of expression was not restricted.

Although in the past, the law has largely dealt with trespassers by way of civil action, the Criminal Justice and Public Order Act 1994 indicated a clear movement towards criminal remedies. This is in keeping with the desire of government to curtail demonstrations. there is a power under s61 to remove trespassers and s.68 which is designed to deal with disruptive trespassers who interfere with lawful activities through disruptive, obstructive or intimidating behaviour by the creation of the offence called 'aggravated trespass'. Section 59 of the Anti-Social Behaviour Act 2003 amends s.68 and

69 of the 1994 Act which extends aggravated trespass to buildings as well as open air.

By s.11 of the Public Order Act 1986, anyone organising a march must give the police six days notice or an offence is committed. This notice must include details of the intended time and route and the address of at least one person proposing to organise it. Sections 12-14 give police powers to impose conditions on processions 'to prevent serious public disorder, serious criminal damage or serious disruption to the life of the community'; ban public processions for up to three months by applying to a local authority for a banning order which needs subsequent confirmation from the Home Secretary; impose conditions on assemblies 'to prevent serious public disorder, serious criminal damage or serious disruption to the life of the community'. the conditions are limited to the specifying of the number of people who may take part, the location of the assembly, and its maximum duration.

The Public Order Act 1986 distinguishes between public processions and public assemblies. Public processions are defined in Flockhart v Robinson (1950) as a body of persons moving along a route. A public assembly was defined in s.16 as an assembly of 20 or more persons in a public place that is wholly or partly open air. However, this has been amended by section 57 of the Anti-Social Behaviour Act 2003 to 2 or more persons.

Section 70 of the 1994 Criminal Justice and Public Order Act introduced a power to ban trespassory assemblies for up to 4 days. These are defined as assemblies which involve at least 20 people, are held on land to which the public has limited or no rights of access and takes place without the permission of the occupier of the land.

Section 71 of the Act gives the police the power to prevent persons proceeding to banned trespassory assemblies.

Breach of the peace

At common law, the police have the power to take whatever action is necessary during a demonstration to prevent a breach of the peace. Not surprisingly, there have been differing views about what exactly constitutes a breach of the peace. 'Breach of the peace' has been defined as being more than a mere disturbance of the public calm or quiet. An element of violence was deemed essential in the case of R. V Howell (1982).

In this case, the appellant, together with others, had been making a disturbance on the street after a party. After complaints made by neighbours the police arrived and told the appellant and the others to leave or be arrested for breach of the peace. The appellant swore several times at two of the policemen who again warned him that he would be arrested for breach of the peace if he did not leave. The appellant continued to swear whereupon one of the police constables took hold of the appellant, but before he could explain why he was arresting the appellant, the appellant struck him in the face and together with the others set on the two policemen. The appellant was convicted of an assault occasioning actual bodily harm on the police constable. He appealed against conviction on the grounds, inter alia, that his arrest was unlawful because no breach of the peace had been proved against him, and accordingly, on the supposition that he had, contrary to his own evidence, struck the police constable, he had been acting lawfully in escaping from a wrongful arrest in that he had used no more force than had been necessary.

Held—(1) A constable or ordinary citizen had power of arrest without warrant where there was a reasonable apprehension of an imminent breach of the peace even though the person arrested had not at that stage committed any breach. Accordingly, there was a power of arrest for breach of the peace where (a) a breach of the peace was committed in the presence of the person making the arrest, or (b) the arrestor reasonably believed that such a breach would be committed in the immediate future by the person arrested even though at the time of the arrest he had not committed any breach, or (c) where a breach had been committed and it was reasonably believed that a renewal of it was threatened. When such a power was exercised on the basis of a belief that a breach of the peace was imminent it had to be established not only that it was an honest, albeit possibly mistaken, belief but that it was a belief which was founded on reasonable grounds.

(2) There could not be a breach of the peace unless an act was done or threatened to be done which either actually harmed a person or, in his presence, his property or was likely to cause such harm or which put someone in fear of such harm being done.

(3) It followed that, in all the circumstances, the appellant had been rightly convicted, and the appeal would accordingly be dismissed.

The violence need not always stem from the demonstrators. In the case of Nicol and Selvanayagam v DPP (1995), demonstrators attempting to disrupt an angling competition by throwing twigs into the water were arrested and subsequently bound over to keep the peace, although no violence or threats of violence had taken place. It was sufficient that their conduct was unreasonable and interfered with lawful activity. A natural consequence of the conduct would be to provoke violence in others.

Conversley, in Redmond-Bate v DPP (1999) the police had arrested three peaceful but vociferous preachers when some members of a crowd gathered round them threatened hostility.

Held: Freedom of speech means nothing unless it includes the freedom to be irritating, contentious, eccentric, heretical, unwelcome and provocative provided it did not tend to provoke violence. There was no reasonable inference available in this case to the police officer that the appellant, preaching about morality, was about to cause a breach of the peace.

This power has been used by the police in a variety of ways: to ask demonstrators to leave the scene, even when acting peacefully (Duncan v Jones 1936); to justify the removal of provocative emblems or banners (Humphries v Connor (1864)); to direct a procession en route if a breach of the preach is reasonably anticipated.

One of the most controversial uses of the power is to prevent demonstrators reaching the scene of the demonstration, a use upheld by the courts. In Moss and Others v Mclachlan (1984) four striking miners were travelling in a convoy of motor vehicles and were stopped by a police cordon at a junction within several miles of four collieries. The inspector in charge believed with reason that a breach of the peace would be committed if they continued to the pits and asked them to turn back. He told them that if they continued they would be obstructing an officer in the execution of his duty and therefore liable to arrest. Many refused to turn back however and, after blocking the road with their vehicles, a group comprising the four striking miners attempted to push their way through the police cordon. They were arrested on the ground that the police feared a breach of the peace at one of the four collieries if the miners had been allowed to proceed. The men were convicted of wilfully obstructing a police officer in the execution of his duty.

Held: The appeal was dismissed: "The situation has to be assessed by the senior police officers present. Provided they honestly and reasonably form the opinion that there is a real risk of a breach of the peace in the sense that it is in close proximity both in place and time, then the conditions exist for reasonable preventive action including, if necessary, the measures taken in this case. . . But, says [counsel], the police can only take preventive action if a breach of the peace is imminent and there was no such imminence here."

In McConnell v Chief Constable of Greater Manchester Police (CA 1990) the Court of Appeal confirmed that a breach of the peace could take place on private premises. If a meeting is held on private premsises it should be noted that the police can insist on entering the premises even against the wishes of the organisers, if they have reasonable grounds to believe that a breach of the peace might occur.

In Thomas v Sawkins (1935) the appellant was one of the conveners of a meeting held to protest against a Bill then before Parliament in a private hall which had been hired for the purpose by one of the other conveners of the meeting. The meeting was extensively advertised and the public were invited to attend it and no charge for admission was made.

The respondent, a police sergeant, and other police officers were refused admission to the hall, but they insisted on entering it and remaining there during the meeting. No criminal offence was committed by any person at the meeting, nor was there any actual breach of the peace or disorder but the respondent and the other officers had reasonable grounds for believing that, if they were not present at the meeting, seditious speeches would be made and that incitements to violence and breaches of the peace would occur.

Held respondent and the other officers were entitled, in the execution of their duty to prevent the commission of any offence or breach of the peace, to enter and remain on the premises.

In Mcleod v MPC (1994) this power was confirmed. The plaintiff, who was divorced from her husband, was ordered by the county court to deliver up certain furniture and effects to the husband. Three days before the expiry of the time limit for complying with the order, the husband went to the plaintiff's house with his brother and sister, a solicitor's clerk and two police officers, whose attendance had been arranged by the husband's solicitors. The plaintiff was not at the house at the time and the door was answered by her mother, who had recently had a stroke. The husband and his brother and sister went into the house and proceeded to load furniture into a van. The plaintiff then arrived on the scene and demanded that the furniture be put back in the house, but one of the police officers insisted that the van was not to be unloaded, that the husband should be allowed to drive away and that any disputes should be sorted out later between the parties' solicitors.

The plaintiff subsequently brought proceedings in the High Court against the police claiming damages for trespass and breach of duty. The judge dismissed the action on the grounds that the police officers had been carrying out their duty to prevent any breach of the peace which they reasonably apprehended might occur and were entitled to enter and remain on private property without the consent of the owner or occupier in carrying out that duty and that they had not participated in the removal or disturbance of the plaintiff's goods.

The plaintiff appealed. Held, at common law the police had power to enter private premises without a warrant to prevent a breach of the peace occurring there if they reasonably believed a breach was likely to occur on the premises, which power was expressly preserved by s17(6)3 of the Police and Criminal Evidence Act 1984. In particular, the police power of entry to prevent a breach of the peace was not restricted to entering premises where public meetings were held.

However, before exercising the power of entry onto private premises, the police had to have a genuine belief that there was a real and imminent risk of a breach of the peace occurring and were required to act with great care and discretion, particularly when exercising the power of entry against the wishes of the owner or occupier of the premises. On the facts, the police officers had a lawful excuse for entering the plaintiff's property. The appeal would therefore be dismissed

The Human Rights Act has had an impact on any such actions to prevent a breach of the peace. In Laporte v The Chief Constable of Gloucestershire (2004) the police detained a coach load of demonstrators en route to an anti-war rally at an RAF base and forced the coach to drive back to London without stopping. It was held that while the police were justified in preventing the demonstrators travelling to the air-base, their actions in escorting the coach back to London went much further than was necessary to prevent a breach of the peace.

Public order offences
The Public Order Act 1986 covers the main public order offences. they are as follows:

- Riot (s.1) " Where 12 or more persons who are present together use or threaten unlawful violence for a common purpose and the conduct of them (taken together) is such as would cause a person of reasonable firmness present at the scene to fear for his personal safety, each of the persons using unlawful violence for the common purpose is guilty of riot".

In order to obtain a conviction, it must be shown that the accused intends to use violence or is aware that his conduct may be violent.

the offence can be committed by aiders and abettors as well as by principals. A conviction has a maximum penalty of ten years.

- Violent disorder (s.2) This is the usual charge for serious outbreaks of public disorder. "Where three or more persons who are present together, use or threaten unlawful violence and the conduct of them (taken together) is such as would cause a person of reasonable firmness present at the scene to fear for his personal safety, each of the persons using or threatening violence is guilty of violent disorder".

Whilst three or more persons must have been present and used or threatened unlawful violence, it is not necessary that three or more persons should actually be charged and prosecuted: (*R v Mahroof* (1988)) (*R v Fleming and Robinson* (1989)). The charge must make clear, however, that the defendant was one of the three or more involved in the commission of the offence.

The expression "present together" does not require any degree of co-operation between those who are using or threatening violence; all that is required is that they be present in the same place at the same time, *R v NW*, CA, 3 March 2010.

- Affray (section 3) This is intended to penalise fighting in that " a person is guilty of affray if he uses or threatens violence towards another and his conduct is such as would cause a person of reasonable firmness present at the scene to fear for his personal safety"

The standard here is whether a hypothetical bystander of reasonable firmness would fear for his safety. In *R v Davison* [1992] the defendant was convicted of affray where he had "swiped" a kitchen knife towards a police officer.. Unlike other offences under the Act the violence must be threatened against the person and must be more than mere threatening words. In *R v Dixon* [1993] the defendant was convicted of affray where he and his Alsatian type dog were pursued by two police officers and cornered in the driveway of a house and he repeated "go on, go on" to the dog who ran forward and bit the police officers. He appealed against the conviction claiming that he had merely used words. the court, while accepting that the offence could not be committed by words alone, dismissed the appeal on the ground that the dog had been used as a weapon.

- **Threatening, abusive and insulting behaviour** (s.4) "a person is guilty of an offence if he:

a) uses towards another person threatening, abusive or insulting words or behaviour, or
b) distributes or displays towards another person any writing, sign...which is threatening, abusive or insulting...with intent to cause another to believe that immediate violence will be used...or to provoke (such) violence.

The consequences feared or provoked must be immediate. Under s. 6(3) a person is guilty of an offence under s.4 only if he intends his words, or behaviour to be threatening, abusive or insulting or is aware that he may be threatening, abusive or insulting. The Act is drafted in such a way to exclude domestic disputes.

Section 4(a) of the Act is designed primarily to deal with serious cases of racial harassment.

- **Offensive conduct** (s.5) "A person is guilty of an offence if he (a) uses threatening, abusive or insulting words or behaviour, or disorderly behaviour, or (b) displays any writing sign or visible representation, which is threatening, abusive or insulting, within the hearing or sight of a person likely to cause harassment alarm or distress thereby."

Section 5(4) gives the police the power of summary arrest for this offence if the person persists in the conduct if warned to stop.

Terrorism

S.1 of the Terrorism Act 2000, as amended by the Terrorism Act 2006, defines terrorism as the use of threat of action involving serious violence against a person; or serious damage to property; or danger to life; or a serious risk to the health and safety of the public; or interference with an electronic system.

The use or threat of action must be designed to influence the government or an international governmental organisation or to intimidate the public or a section of the public. The use or threat of action must be made for the purpose of advancing a political, religious or ideological cause.

The Terrorism Act 2000 made it illegal for certain terrorist groups to operate in the UK. The groups listed are prescribed organisations and include international terrorist groups. The police were given wider powers under the Act, including wider stop and search powers and the power to detain suspects after arrest for up to 28 days, although periods of over two days must be approved by a magistrate. This period was extended to 28 days by the Terrorism Act 2006. A number of new offences were introduced under the 2006 Act allowing the police to arrest people suspected of inciting terrorist acts, seeking or providing training for terrorist purposes at home or overseas and providing instruction or training in the use of firearms, explosives, or chemical, biological or nuclear weapons.

The Anti-Terrorism, Crime and Security Act 2001 aimed to cut off terrorist funding and also to ensure that government departments and agencies can collect and share information required for countering the terrorist threat. Immigration procedures were streamlined and other security measures introduced.

The Prevention of Terrorism Act 2005 introduced control orders, which impose conditions on where a person can go and what they can do. These must be signed by the Home Secretary and confirmed by a judge within seven days. A control order may impose conditions banning possession or use of specific articles or substances, and prohibit the use of services such at the internet. An order can also control a persons place of residence and travel movements.

A control order may also contain a specific 24hr ban on movements and requirements to surrender a passport and give access to specified people to his home including officials searching his home with a power to remove items. A person subject to a control order may also be tagged, and be forced to report to a specified place at a specified time.

Counter Terrorism Act 2008

This Act amends the law on terrorism in several ways. Its provisions affect the gathering and sharing of information for, among other things, counter terrorism purposes. This includes the disclosure and sharing of information with the security services. It also makes provisions relevant to the post-charge questioning of terrorism suspects, the prosecution and sentencing of those charged with terrorism offences, the financial aspects of terrorism, sensitive information and the creation of new powers and offences relating to terrorism.

The Counter Terrorism and Security Act 2015

The Counter-Terrorism and Security Act contains powers to help the UK respond to the threat of terrorism. It received Royal Assent on 12 February 2015. The act will:

- disrupt the ability of people to travel abroad to engage in terrorist activity and then return to the UK
- enhance the ability of operational agencies to monitor and control the actions of those who pose a threat
- combat the underlying ideology that feeds, supports and sanctions terrorism

Ch.12

Judicial Review and Administrative Law

Judicial review-an overview

If an individual has suffered, or thinks they have suffered, a grievance at the hands of a public body then he or she may be able to obtain redress through the courts. Quite apart from any statutory right of appeal, there may be a right to invoke the inherent supervisory jurisdiction of the High Court. This jurisdiction enables the court to review the decisions of government ministers, the inferior courts, tribunals and other administrative bodies to ensure that they do not act illegally or irrationally. The courts are not challenging the relative merits of the decision but are looking to see whether it is a decision that the body is entitled to make.

Historically, the basis of the courts intervention was the *ultra vires* doctrine. This means that if a body acts beyond its powers then the courts can intervene. This can occur in a number of ways. The body might be exercising the wrong powers or taking the wrong decision. In Att-Gen v Fulham Corporation (1921) the local authority had powers under the Baths and Wash Houses Acts 1846-1878 to establish baths and wash houses and bathing spaces generally. The courts held that this did not give it the power to operate a commercial laundry. Basically, courts have to consider what is the area over which power is given and any exercise of power which falls outside of that area will be *ultra vires*.

The doctrine of *ultra vires* is used to control the way power is used, as well as the scope of that power. Where a body uses its powers in an obviously unfair way, or unreasonable manner, acts in bad faith, the courts would intervene on the grounds that the body had abused its powers.

An important case here is Anisminic v Foreign Compensation Commission (1969). The Foreign Compensation Commission was set up by an Act of Parliament that provided that 'The determination by the Commission of any application made to them under this Act shall not be called in question in any court of law'. The Commission rejected Anisminic's application for compensation, and the company sought a declaration that the decision was unlawful. Their argument was simply that the Commission misinterpreted the criteria for compensation, yet the House of Lords issued the declaration. The majority (3-2) of the Law Lords held that the Commission had misinterpreted the criteria, and that their error of law was of such a kind that there was no 'determination' at all. According to Lord Reid, the Commission had decided the claim 'on a ground which they had no right to take into account' and as a result their decision was not a determination, but a nullity.

What is administrative law?

Administrative (or public) law is generally concentrated on the control of the Government (or public authorities). Wade and Forsyth have indicated that:

"The primary purpose of administrative law [...] is to keep the powers of government within their legal bounds, so as to protect the citizen against their abuse. The powerful engines of authority must be prevented from running amok".

This control is sometimes affected by use of the courts and judicial review provides one (of a number) of legal controls on administrative actions.

The 2000 edition of the Treasury Solicitors' publication, *The Judge Over Your Shoulder* provides a useful description of who is affected by administrative law indicating that:

1.2 "Administrative" or "public" law governs the acts of public bodies and the exercise of public functions. Public bodies include "non-departmental public bodies", such as the Committee on Standards in Public Life, and Next Steps Agencies like HM Prison Service.

1.3 Private sector bodies may also be subject to administrative law when they exercise a public function. Generally, bodies exercise public functions when they act and have authority to act for the collective benefit of the general public. The activities of City institutions with market regulatory functions, like the London Stock Exchange, are a good example.

The recently published Fourth Edition of the publication goes on to add that:

"the Human Rights Act 1998 is part of administrative law because it governs the exercise of statutory powers by public authorities. For example, the Act has an important bearing on the way in which those powers are to be interpreted. The devolution legislation is part of administrative law for the same reason. Likewise European Community (EC) law may be relevant to the exercise of statutory powers".

Judicial Review

As stated at the opening of the chapter, judicial review is a High Court procedure for challenging administrative actions. Delegated legislation may also be challenged. It allows individuals, businesses or groups to challenge in court the lawfulness of decisions taken by

Ministers, Government Departments and other public bodies. These bodies include local authorities, the immigration authorities, and regulatory bodies (such as OFCOM and the OFGEM) and some tribunals. In the case of *R v HM the Queen in Council, ex parte Vijayatunga*, Mr Justice Simon Brown observed that "judicial review is the exercise of the court's inherent power at common law to determine whether action is lawful or not; in a word to uphold the rule of law".

Her Majesty's Courts Service indicates that:
The supervisory jurisdiction [of the Administrative court], exercised in the main through the procedure of Judicial Review, covers persons or bodies exercising a public law function - a wide and still growing field.

In the case of *Council of Civil Service Unions v Minister for the Civil Service* [1985] AC 374 (often referred to as the *GCHQ* case), Lord Diplock observed that:

The subject matter of every judicial review is a decision made by some person or (body of persons) whom I shall call the 'decision maker' or else a refusal by him to make a decision.

The Fourth Edition of *The Judge Over Your Shoulder* provides a helpful analysis of what constitutes a "decision":

Administrative law (and the Court procedure called Judicial Review) is said to govern the making of "decisions" by public authorities, and the application of decision-making procedures. "Decisions" typically relate to a particular matter actually affecting an individual person or group. Examples are: the grant of a planning application to an individual or company; the determination of a person's immigration status; the allocation of a school place; assigning a prisoner to a particular security category. The scope of administrative law does however go wider than "decisions" of this direct kind: the Courts have held that Judicial Review extends to subordinate legislation, and things like policies (of general application), reports and recommendations, and advice or guidance.

This is not an exhaustive list. For example the court also has the power to act when an authority fails to reach a decision – Rule 54.1(2)(a)(ii) of the *Civil Procedure Rules* ("the CPR") provides that a claim for judicial review includes a "failure to act in relation to the exercise of a public function".

The Administrative Court Office has published a description of when the use of judicial review is appropriate, noting that:

Judicial review is the procedure by which you can seek to challenge the decision, action, or failure to act of a public body such as a government department or a local authority or other body exercising a public law function. If you are challenging the decision of a court, the jurisdiction of judicial review extends only to decisions of inferior courts. It does not extend to decisions of the High Court or Court of Appeal. Judicial review must be used where you are seeking:

- a mandatory order (i.e. an order requiring the public body to do something and formerly known as an order of mandamus);
- a prohibiting order (i.e. an order preventing the public body from doing something and formerly known as an order of prohibition); or
- a quashing order (i.e. an order quashing the public body's decision and formerly known as an order of certiorari);
- a declaration;

- Human Rights Act Damages.

Claims will generally be heard by a single Judge sitting in open Court at the Royal Courts of Justice in London. They may be heard by a Divisional Court (a court of two judges) where the Court so directs. The court is now referred to as the Administrative Court. Prior to 2000, judicial review cases were heard by High Court judges sitting in the Crown Office List. The Administrative Court is part of the Queen's Bench Division of the High Court. In strict terms the Administrative Court refers to the list of judges authorised by the Lord Chief Justice to sit on Administrative law cases. HM Court Services indicates that:

Judges are nominated by the Lord Chief Justice to sit on Administrative cases. There are presently 37 judges, including judges of the Chancery Division and of the Family Division who act as additional judges of the Queen's Bench Division when dealing with Administrative Court cases.

1. The limits of the Administrative Court's role and the *Wednesbury* principle

Judicial review is not concerned with the 'merits' of a decision or whether the public body has made the 'right' decision. The only question before the court is whether the body has acted unlawfully. In particular, it is not the task of the courts to substitute its judgment for that of the decision maker. The courts would traditionally only intervene where a public body had used a power for a purpose not allowed by the legislation (acting *ultra vires*) or in circumstances where when using its powers, the body has acted in a manner that was obviously unreasonable or irrational. In cases where there is a real unfairness, the courts may now be willing to intervene where the public body has made a serious factual error in reaching its decision. In the case of *Associated Provincial Picture*

Houses Ltd v Wednesbury Corp in 1948, Lord Greene MR set out the circumstances in which the courts would intervene. The case is of such historical importance a substantial excerpt of Lord Greene's judgment is set out below:

What, then, is the power of the courts? They can only interfere with an act of executive authority if it be shown that the authority has contravened the law. It is for those who assert that the [...] authority has contravened the law to establish that proposition [...] It is not to be assumed prima facie that responsible bodies like the local authority in this case will exceed their powers; but the court, whenever it is alleged that the local authority have contravened the law, must not substitute itself for that authority. It is only concerned with seeing whether or not the proposition is made good. When an executive discretion is entrusted by Parliament to a body such as the local authority in this case, what appears to be an exercise of that discretion can only be challenged in the courts in a strictly limited class of case. As I have said, it must always be remembered that the court is not a court of appeal. When discretion of this kind is granted the law recognizes certain principles upon which that discretion must be exercised, but within the four corners of those principles the discretion, in my opinion, is an absolute one and cannot be questioned in any court of law. What then are those principles?

They are well understood. They are principles which the court looks to in considering any question of discretion of this kind. The exercise of such a discretion must be a real exercise of the discretion. If, in the statute conferring the discretion, there is to be found expressly or by implication matters which the authority exercising the discretion ought to have regard to, then in exercising the discretion it must have regard to those matters. Conversely, if the nature of the subject matter and the general interpretation of the

Act make it clear that certain matters would not be germane to the matter in question, the authority must disregard those irrelevant collateral matters [...] I am not sure myself whether the permissible grounds of attack cannot be defined under a single head. It has been perhaps a little bit confusing to find a series of grounds set out. Bad faith, dishonesty - those of course, stand by themselves - unreasonableness, attention given to extraneous circumstances, disregard of public policy and things like that have all been referred to, according to the facts of individual cases, as being matters which are relevant to the question. If they cannot all be confined under one head, they at any rate, I think, overlap to a very great extent. For instance, we have heard in this case a great deal about the meaning of the word "unreasonable." It is true the discretion must be exercised reasonably.

What does that mean? Lawyers familiar with the phraseology commonly used in relation to exercise of statutory discretions often use the word "unreasonable" in a rather comprehensive sense. It has frequently been used and is frequently used as a general description of the things that must not be done. For instance, a person entrusted with a discretion must, so to speak, direct himself properly in law. He must call his own attention to the matters which he is bound to consider.

He must exclude from his consideration matters which are irrelevant to what he has to consider. If he does not obey those rules, he may truly be said, and often is said, to be acting "unreasonably." Similarly, there may be something so absurd that no sensible person could ever dream that it lay within the powers of the authority. Warrington L.J. in Short v. Poole Corporation [1926] gave the example of the red-haired teacher, dismissed because she had red hair. That is unreasonable in one sense. In another sense it is taking into consideration extraneous matters. It is so unreasonable that it might almost be described as being done in bad faith; and, in fact, all these things run into one another.

2. A relaxation of the *Wednesbury* principle?

Subsequent case law, can be seen to have "loosened" the *Wednesbury* test. *Fordham's Judicial Review Handbook* argues that "the most popular broad classification of judicial review grounds is Lord Diplock's *GCHQ* threefold division, into illegality, (unlawfulness), irrationality (unreasonableness) and procedural impropriety (unfairness)". He states that "judicial review has come a long way since 1948." In *R v Secretary of State for the Environment, ex p Nottinghamshire County Council* [1986] AC 240 Lord Scarman explicitly indicated that Wednesbury was not an exhaustive statement of the law, noting that:

'Wednesbury principles' is a convenient legal 'shorthand' used by lawyers to refer to the classical review by Lord Greene MR in the Wednesbury case of the circumstances in which the courts will intervene to quash as being illegal the exercise of an administrative discretion. No question of constitutional propriety arose in the case, and the Master of the Rolls was not concerned with the constitutional limits to the exercise of judicial power in our parliamentary democracy. There is a risk, however, that the judgment of the Master of the Rolls may be treated as a complete, exhaustive, definitive statement of the law.

In the case of *Council of Civil Service Unions v Minister for the Civil Service* (a case concerning the lawfulness of the union ban at GCHQ and therefore generally referred to as the *GCHQ* case) Lord Diplock attempted to set out the main grounds for judicial review in a modern way:

Judicial review has I think developed to a stage today when, without reiterating any analysis of the steps by which the development has come about, one can conveniently classify under three heads the grounds on which administrative action is subject to control by judicial review. The first ground I would call 'illegality', the second 'irrationality' and the third 'procedural impropriety'. That is not to say that further development on a case by case basis may not in the course of time add further grounds. I have in mind particularly the possible adoption in the future of the principle of 'proportionality' which is recognised in the administrative law of several of our fellow members of the European Economic Community [...]

Dividing the grounds for judicial review into the *GCHQ* categories, further subcategories emerge. Grounds that are now considered acceptable to bring claims for judicial review include:

1. Illegality

In the *GCHQ* case, Lord Diplock confirmed that "by illegality as a ground for judicial review I mean that the decision maker must understand correctly the law that regulates his decision-making power and must give effect to it. Whether he has or not is par excellence a justiciable question". A number of examples of illegality are listed below.

a. Decision maker acting ultra vires

As we have seen above, when a body is described as acting *ultra vires* it is acting beyond its prescribed powers. An action can be *ultra vires* where it the body has taken an action which is incompatible with a higher legal authority (such as EC legislation or domestic primary or subordinate legislation).

Difficulties in this area can also arise where a body is using a statutory power for a collateral purpose (namely one which is alien to the purpose for which it was granted).

Where a body (such as a local authority) is exercising a power where the statute under which it acts has set out a particular prescribed procedure, if the procedure is not followed, this may (in some circumstances) also make the action *ultra vires*.

b. Unlawfully delegating power or fettering discretion

A public body is not entitled either to improperly delegate its powers or to act under a completely inflexible policy. In particular, while it is accepted that Ministers cannot personally make every decision issued in their name where legislation confers a power on a specified individual or body, the power cannot be delegated to another person or body.

Moreover, a body or tribunal is not entitled blindly to follow policy guidelines. Neither is it entitled to fetter the exercise of its discretion. In the case of *Port of London Authority, ex p Kynoch Ltd* Lord Justice Banks observed that:

There are on the one hand, cases where a tribunal in the honest exercise of its discretion has adopted a policy, and without refusing to hear an applicant intimates what its policy is, and that after hearing him it will in accordance with its policy decide against him, unless there is something exceptional in his case [...]

On the other hand there are cases where a tribunal has passed a rule, or come to a determination, not to hear any application of a particular character by whomsoever made.

It is this latter course of action which is not acceptable. In the more recent case of *R v Secretary of State for the Home Department, ex p Venables*, Lord Browne-Wilkenson observed that:

When Parliament confers a discretionary power exercisable from time to time over a period, such a power must be exercised on each occasion in the light of the circumstances at that time. In consequence, the person on whom the power is conferred cannot fetter the future exercise of his discretion by committing himself now as to the way he will exercise the power in the future [...] By the same token, the person on whom the power has been conferred cannot fetter the way he will use that power by ruling out of consideration on the future exercise of that power factors which may then be relevant to such an exercise. These considerations do not preclude the person on whom the power is conferred from developing and applying a policy as to the approach which he will adopt in the generality of case [...] But the position is different if the policy adopted is such as to preclude the person on whom the power is conferred from departing from the policy or from taking into account circumstances which are relevant to the particular case [...] If such an inflexible and invariable policy is adopted, both the policy and the decision taken pursuant to it will be unlawful.

c. Taking into account irrelevant considerations

A claim for judicial review can lie where a body or tribunal has either disregarded a relevant consideration, or taken into account an irrelevant consideration when reaching a decision. In the case of *R (on the application of Alconbury Developments Ltd) v Secretary of State for the Environment, Transport and the Regions* Lord Slynn observed that:

It has long been established that if the Secretary of State [...] takes into account matters irrelevant to his decision or refuses or fails to take account of matters relevant to his decision, or reaches a perverse decision, the court may set his decision aside.

2. Irrationality

In the *GCHQ* case, Lord Diplock observed that:

> By 'irrationality' I mean what can now be succinctly referred to as 'Wednesbury unreasonableness' [...] it applies to a decision which is so outrageous in its defiance of logic or of accepted moral standards that no sensible person who had his mind to the question to be decided could have arrived at it. Whether a decision falls within this category is a question that judges by their training and experience should be well equipped to answer, or else there would be something badly wrong with our judicial system.

a. The obligation to act reasonably

As mentioned above, it is not the task of the courts to substitute its judgment for that of the decision maker and accordingly, the courts will only interfere on a matter of reasonableness when the claimant is able to provide a strong clear case. *The Judge Over Your Shoulder* states that "reasonable":

> Is not the same as saying [a] decision must be absolutely correct or that the Court would necessarily have made the same decision. It means that in making the decision you must apply logical or rational principles. If a decision is challenged, the Court will examine the decision to see whether it was made according to logical principles, and will often expressly disavow any intention to substitute its own decision for that of the decision maker [...] There are sound practical, as well as legal/constitutional reasons for the Court adopting this "hands off" approach: the decision maker may be aware of policy implications or other aspects of the public interest which are not obvious to the Court.

3. Procedural Impropriety

Complaints can also be made, not merely in respect of the decision taken, but the procedure by which the decision was made. Some examples are listed below:

a. Failure to give each party to a dispute an opportunity to be heard

Where a body or tribunal is determining a dispute, it is obliged to give each party a fair opportunity to put their case.

b. Bias

While actual bias is rare, the court will also be seeking to examine whether there has been an appearance of bias. The case of *Magill v Porter* [2001] (in which Lord Hope observed that: "The question is whether the fair minded observer, having considered the facts, would conclude that there was a real possibility that the tribunal was biased") provides a good example of the test that will be used.

c. Failure to conduct a consultation properly

Where a consultation exercise is undertaken by a public body, it must be conducted properly. The Cabinet Office has produced a *Code of Practice on Written Consultations* indicating that "Government departments should carry out a full public consultation whenever options are being considered for a new policy or if new regulation is planned".

In the case of *R v North and East Devon Health Authority, ex p Coughlan* the Court of Appeal determined that:

To be proper, consultation must be undertaken at a time when proposals are still at a formative stage; it must include sufficient reasons for particular proposals to allow those consulted to give intelligent consideration and an intelligent response; adequate time must be given for this purpose; and the product of consultation must be consciously taken into account when the ultimate decision is taken.

d. Failure to give adequate reasons

Challenges to "reasons" are commonly heard in the Administrative Court. The main ways in which a duty to give reasons can arise has been considered in Fordham's *Judicial Review Handbook* which concludes that it arises: where it is expressly required in legislation; where it is called for in fairness, under the duty of candour owed by a body under challenge; and, where a response which is unreasoned may be seen as unreasonable.

The Divisional Court considered the position in relation to the existence of a duty to give reasons in the case of *R v Ministry of Defence, ex parte Murray.* It recognised that while the law did not at present recognise a general duty to give reasons, there was a perceptible trend towards an insistence on greater openness in the making of administrative decisions.

Where reasons are required from a body (for example when a tribunal makes a determination, or a planning authority reaches a decision on the merits of a planning appeal), "it is required to give reasons which are proper, adequate and intelligible and enable the person affected to know why they have won or lost."

e. Legitimate expectation

The doctrine of legitimate expectation addresses circumstances in which a decision maker may have operated a practice or made a promise that raised expectations that it would be unfair or unreasonable to dishonour. Whether a legitimate expectation has arisen (and whether it can be overridden) will depend on a number of factors.

The Judge Over Your Shoulder suggests that these include:
Whether the words or conduct which gave rise to the expectation were clear and unequivocal,

Whether the person who promised the benefit had the legal power to grant it (or whether he was acting *ultra vires*), and;

Whether the recipient of the promise took action in reliance upon it to their detriment. Wade and Forsyth suggest that the doctrine has developed both in the context of reasonableness and in the context of natural justice. It is also a fundamental principle of EC law.

The above list, however, should in no way be taken as a comprehensive record of the traditional grounds under which a claimant could pursue a challenge. Moreover, it is important to note that commentators consider that while they have "aged well "the *GCHQ* grounds are neither exhaustive nor mutually exclusive.

Other potential challenges

In addition to the above grounds, the use of a power may also be unlawful if the effect of the decision is to contravene a claimant's rights under the European Convention on Human Rights, or his rights under EC law.

1. The *Human Rights Act 1998*

The preamble to the *Human Rights Act 1998* indicates that it will "give further effect to the rights and freedoms guaranteed under the *European Convention on Human Rights"* Prior to the implementation of the *Human Rights Act*, while the judiciary would try to interpret legislation in line with Convention obligations, the limits of statutory interpretation could be reached in cases where there was a clear cut conflict between the wording of the domestic law and the requirements of the Convention. In the case of *Taylor v Co-operative Retail Services (1982)* Lord Denning described the dilemma, noting that:

Mr Taylor was subjected to a degree of compulsion which was contrary to the freedom guaranteed by the European Convention on Human Rights. He was dismissed by his employers because he refused to join a trade union which operated the 'closed shop'. He cannot recover any compensation from his employer under English Law because under the Acts of 1974 and 1976, his dismissal is to be regarded as fair. But those Acts themselves are inconsistent with the freedom guaranteed by the European Convention. The UK Government is responsible for passing those Acts and should pay him compensation. He can recover it by applying to the European Commission and thence to the European Court of Human Rights [...] He cannot recover compensation in these courts. But if he applies to the ECHR, he may in the long run – and I am afraid it may be a long run – obtain compensation there. So in the end justice may be done. But not here.

Following the entry into force of the Act, victims of unlawful acts by public authorities were able to raise Convention issues in the domestic courts.

Judicial Review-Remedies
The following remedies may be claimed only by judicial review:

Quashing order
The court examines the defendant public authorities proceedings. If there is any illegality, irrationality or procedural impropriety its decision has no legal effect.

Mandatory order
This is an order to do something as the law requires.

Prohibiting order

This is an order not to do something or to discontinue doing something which is unlawful.

The following remedies may be claimed by judicial review procedure:

An injunction-these may be mandatory or prohibitive.

A declaration-this is a statement declaring whether something the defendant public authority has done or is about to do is unlawful. Section 4 Human Rights Act 1998 gives the High Court in England and Wales the jurisdiction to state whether a statute is compatible with Convention rights.

Damages in conjunction with any other remedy available by judicial review

Part 54 Civil Procedure rules provides that a claim for judicial review may include a claim for damages, restitution, or the recovery of a sum due but a claimant may not seek such a remedy alone.

****

Index

www.straightforwardco.co.uk

All titles, listed below, in the Straightforward Guides Series can be purchased online, using credit card or other forms of payment by going to www.straightfowardco.co.uk A discount of 25% per title is offered with online purchases.

Law
A Straightforward Guide to:
Consumer Rights
Bankruptcy Insolvency and the Law
Employment Law
Private Tenants Rights
Family law
Small Claims in the County Court
Contract law
Intellectual Property and the law
Divorce and the law
Leaseholders Rights
The Process of Conveyancing
Knowing Your Rights and Using the Courts
Producing Your own Will
Housing Rights
The Bailiff the law and You
Probate and The Law
Company law
What to Expect When You Go to Court
Guide to Competition Law
Give me Your Money-Guide to Effective Debt Collection
Caring for a Disabled Child

General titles
Letting Property for Profit
Buying, Selling and Renting property

Buying a Home in England and France
Bookkeeping and Accounts for Small Business
Creative Writing
Freelance Writing
Writing Your own Life Story
Writing performance Poetry
Writing Romantic Fiction
Speech Writing
Teaching Your Child to Read and write
Teaching Your Child to Swim
Raising a Child-The Early Years
Creating a Successful Commercial Website
The Straightforward Business Plan
The Straightforward C.V.
Successful Public Speaking
Handling Bereavement
Play the Game-A Compendium of Rules
Individual and Personal Finance
Understanding Mental Illness
The Two Minute Message
Guide to Self Defence
Buying a Used Car
Tiling for Beginners

Go to:

www.straightforwardco.co.uk

Ce livre est imprimé sur
du papier contenant plus
de 50% de papier recyclé
dont 10% de fibres recyclées.

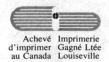

Achevé   Imprimerie
d'imprimer Gagné Ltée
au Canada Louiseville